T0328183

This book examines alternative methods for achieving optimality without all the apparatus of economic planning (such as information retrieval, computation of solutions, and separate implementation systems), or a vain reliance on sufficiently "perfect" competition. All rely entirely on the self-interest of economic agents and voluntary contract. The author considers methods involving feed-back iterative controls which require the prior selection of a "criterion function," but no prior calculation of optimal quantities. The target is adjusted as the results for each step become data for the criterion function. Implementation is built in by the incentive structure, and all controls rely on consistency with the self-interest of individuals. The applicability of all the methods is shown to be independent of the form of ownership of enterprises: examples are given for industries which are wholly privately owned, wholly nationalized, mixed, and labor-managed.

Information, incentives and the economics of control

Information, incentives and the economics of control

G.C. ARCHIBALD

Department of Economics,
University of British Columbia

CAMBRIDGE
UNIVERSITY PRESS

CAMBRIDGE UNIVERSITY PRESS
Cambridge, New York, Melbourne, Madrid, Cape Town, Singapore, São Paulo

Cambridge University Press
The Edinburgh Building, Cambridge CB2 2RU, UK

Published in the United States of America by Cambridge University Press, New York

www.cambridge.org
Information on this title: www.cambridge.org/9780521330459

First published 1992
This digitally printed first paperback version 2005

A catalogue record for this publication is available from the British Library

Library of Congress Cataloguing in Publication data

Archibald, G.C., 1926–
    Information, incentives, and the economics of control / G.C.
Archibald.
        p. cm.
    Includes index.
    ISBN 0 521 33045 9 (hardback)
    1. Mathematical optimization.   2. Economic man.   3. Consumers'
preferences.   4. Competition.   I. Title.
HB143.7.A73 1992
330'.01'1–dc20 91-43850 CIP

ISBN-13 978-0-521-33045-9 hardback
ISBN-10 0-521-33045-9 hardback

ISBN-13 978-0-521-02279-8 paperback
ISBN-10 0-521-02279-7 paperback

To the memory of my father

Contents

Preface

A preface is perhaps a place to offer some explanation, and certainly a place to make acknowledgements and offer thanks.

The only part of this book which may, I think, require some explanation is Part II, and the explanation is not independent of some debts I wish to acknowledge. When I was an undergraduate at the London School of Economics the works of Oscar Lange and Abba Lerner were on the reading list, and, true to the liberal and open tradition of the School, "socialist economics" was prominent on the agenda. Later, when I was on the teaching staff of the School, I encountered the work of Karl Popper and some of his colleagues, as well as that of the great, if misguided, Bill Phillips. It was not until I had been for some years at this University that I realized that a feed-back, or iterative, control system might be designed in such a fashion as to avoid some of the difficulties inherent both in Phillips' control systems and in central planning. Such a system requires the prior selection of what I call a Criterion Function. Such a function must have the properties that it signals clearly, probably by reaching an extremum, that the target has been reached, and sufficient information to estimate its value must be generated during the iterative process itself. Given these properties, there would be no need for a planning procedure: no need, that is, to collect sufficient information to calculate optimal quantities, or prices, in advance. Clearly, the iterative control process has itself to be incentive-compatible at every step, and strategy-proof. If, then, it is properly designed, the means of implementation are not to be considered as a separate step, as they are when the target is the outcome of a planning procedure. Errors, of course, operate in real time, and impose costs, as do errors in a process of market adjustment. I do not know how to estimate the costs of these errors, nor how to compare them with the adjustment costs of other systems.

Lerner's *The Economics of Control* left the problems of information and incentives quite unresolved, and this work may be regarded as, in part, an attempt to fill up some of the gaps he left (my title is a deliberate echo of his). Nonetheless, the use of iterative control systems in no way supposes state ownership. Examples in Part II are deliberately chosen to illustrate their use in cases of pure private ownership, public ownership, and mixed cases. This book is thus not intended as a contribution only to the "economics of socialism."

With these considerations in mind, I have, in Part II, provided what amounts to a "DIY manual" for the construction of feed-back control systems with desirable properties. All depends, however, on the choice of Criterion Function. In a Second-Best world, the justification of a Criterion Function may not be at all easy. I have accordingly offered a Second-Best example, but this depends on a brutal aggregation of consumers' preferences. It is sadly possible that the DIY kit serves no useful purpose.

Parts III and IV of this book require, I think no particular explanation. They are variations of the theme "control," in the interests of efficiency (and perhaps equity) without planning, but requiring the construction of appropriate institutions that allow the solution to be reached by voluntary contract rather than by command.

My remaining debts are too heavy to be fully acknowledged. I hope the many individuals who have contributed to my knowledge and understanding will forgive me for not listing them. (One chapter, indeed, was first written as a partial reply to a question posed by a conspicuously intelligent and able graduate student; I shall not even name him.) I clearly must identify and thank former collaborators who have permitted me to use our joint work here, and even read and commented on my use of it: Russell Davidson, David Donaldson, and Hugh Neary.

I take pleasure in thanking several cohorts of graduate students who have patiently permitted me to try my ideas on them.

I am much indebted to the Canada Council for a Killam Research Fellowship during my tenure of which I was able to make coherent some of the material offered here. This University has given me the sabbatical leaves I needed for the writing, and the Social Science and Humanities Research Council of Canada has been generous with research grants and leave fellowships. My greatest single debt must, however, be to the Economics Department of this University, which has invariably provided both the atmosphere of challenge and friendly criticism, and practical support.

Ms. Marissa Relova somehow deciphered my handwriting and typed the whole text, and dealt patiently with my innumerable corrections and revisions.

My wife has had to put up for several years with a degree of preoccupation and abstraction sadly beyond the licensed "absent mindedness" of professors.

G.C.A.
University of British Columbia
September 1991

Part I

Introductory

1

Two preliminary matters

1.1 Individualism and holism

It has long been usual to find, at the beginning of a work on welfare economics, a statement to the effect "I adopt the liberal principle that individual preferences are to count: take it or leave it." I indeed adopt this principle here; but I think that some justification may be in order. Nothing like a complete justification can be attempted: that would require a major work of political philosophy. Nonetheless, we may consider one alternative to individualism, and some difficulties.

In common speech, we often use collectives such as "France," "the working class," or the "elderly." These collectives may be – perhaps usually are – employed simply as shorthand for aggregates of individuals. They may, however, mean more than this. It may be believed that the collective, the group or "whole," is an entity, and actually exists in its own right. Philosophers call this view "methodological holism." There are many versions of holism. The version most obviously antithetical to individualism was identified by Popper (1957), and most sharply defined by Agassi (1960). The key is his Proposition 4: "*If* 'wholes' exist, then they have distinct aims and interests of their own." This is, perhaps, frightening. A holist in this sense may talk, for instance, of the "interest of the state," or the "national interest," without at all intending by these terms merely a shorthand for certain collections of individuals. The liberal alternative adopted by most economists is, of course, "methodological individualism."

It is not my purpose to try to persuade on this matter. I shall say only that if the choice is between individualism and holism as defined by Agassi, perhaps few of us will hesitate. We should, however, be aware that we are making a *choice*, and that it is perhaps as difficult to give a rational argument for such a philosophical choice as for any faith. We should also notice that we have to be very careful about the meaning of some convenient terms, such as "the interests of the Third World." We need not, however, become so timid as to eschew entirely the use of collective terms: whether the intent is holist or individualist is usually evident from the context. (I say "usually," not "always." Whether or not Marx, for instance, was a holist in Agassi's sense may not always be entirely obvious.)

If one adopts individualism as one's methodology, choices still remain. The social scientist may adopt it for both positive and normative purposes. If he adopts it for both, he immediately faces another problem: is it *sufficient*? Is he, that is, willing to become a monist in his ethics, believing not only that individual preferences count, but that *only* they count, or should count, in decisions on economic or social policy? Clearly, the choice of individualism over holism does not itself entail monism. Nonetheless, one monist philosophy commands attention. The methodological individualist has somehow to deal with the problem of aggregating individual preferences. Utilitarianism offers a comprehensive and sufficient solution to that problem. The individualist who is not a utilitarian really has no solution to offer, as we know from the work of Arrow (see particularly his 1951b). Yet there are individualists, of whom I am one, who cannot accept monist utilitarianism, and must be content with what Brian Barry has somewhere called a "pluralist cocktail" of ethical principles (which does not entail giving no weight to any utilitarian argument).[1]

This is, of course, not a book on ethics, and much of the discourse is strictly positive. Yet in even a work on the implementation of welfare economics rather than on welfare economics *per se*, it seems that some reason for taking the subject seriously, or at least advertising the author's methodological choices, may be appropriate. And when we consider extended preferences, in ch. 2 below, we shall find that we may want to ask if some preferences should *not* count.

1.2 Incentive compatibility

It is consistent with a positive individualist methodology to assume that economic agents act entirely, or mainly, for motives of self-interest, although this is not entailed. Indeed, in ch. 2 I investigate extended preferences – assuming, that is, that the agent explicitly takes into consideration the wellbeing of some, or all, of his fellow citizens. We shall find that, on apparently quite "reasonable" restrictions, these preferences are perfectly consistent with standard "liberal" results and policies: agents will for the most part behave as ordinary selfish maximizers. This in turn implies that, in considering any methods for "control" of the economy, incentive compatibility must be taken seriously.

We owe to Adam Smith the insight that matters go more smoothly if institutions are such that private and social interest coincide. D.H. Robertson (1956) put it clearly. "What do economists economize on?," he asked. This was not a rhetorical question. His answer was: Love. He explained that love is scarce, and that it is wasteful to depend on it for everyday social arrangements that depend, or can be made to depend, simply on self-interest. As Smith (1776) put it "It is not from the benevolence of the butcher, the brewer, or the baker that we expect our dinner, but from their regard to their own interest. We address ourselves not to their humanity but to their self love, and we talk to them not of our necessity, but of their advantages" (p. 14).

If we economize on love, we do more: we economize on policemen. If it is in the interest of agents to do what is socially desirable, we have neither to appeal to their altruism nor employ policemen to ensure their good behavior. Institutions that economize on polcemen also economize on something else expensive: information. If it is in agents' interests to "do the right thing," there is no need to use resources to find out just what they are doing, or how.

The standard formulation of the principal–agent problem is precisely as a problem in economizing on information, love, and policemen. It is assumed that all concerned are exclusively self-interested, and that lack of information entirely precludes monitoring of the agent. Yet there is a problem here. May not an agent himself become the principal in some subsidiary con- tract(s) that tend to subvert the object of the original contract (see Eswaran and Kotwal, 1984)? The possibility of side- payments suggests that agents may indeed become principals, and vice versa: the old *quis custodiet* question leads to an infinite regress.[2] I do not presume to offer any general conclusion on this matter. Notice that *any* social institution, existing or proposed, has at least an implicit incentive structure which requires examination, usually more for its unintended than for its intended consequences. And suppose that we do encounter, if not a demonstrably infinite regress, at least a tediously long chain of possibilities for side-payments and subversion: what do we do? Sooner or later, exhaustion sets in. We may also notice that in any such chain, perhaps at the first step, we shall encounter conduct regarded in many societies as immoral, and possibly illegal. If our object is to economize on policemen, that is not a sufficient excuse for terminating our enquiry: if the incentives to "misbehavior" are large enough, the jails will not be; and, in any case, policemen are but agents, and agents who may become principals.

The policy I have followed in this book is to pursue the possibilities of strategic behavior, and of side payments (agents becoming principals) as far as my own ingenuity and energy permit (and obviously no further). In at least two places, I have had to give up, and appeal for criminal sanctions. I can only warn the reader to be alert to possibilities that I have overlooked, or inadequately investigated.

2

Extended preferences[1]

2.1 The axiom of selfishness and the Two Theorems of Welfare Economics

The preferences attributed to individuals in welfare economics are usually assumed to satisfy the *axiom of selfishness* – that is, each individual is assumed to order consumption bundles for himself without regard to anyone else's preferences or actual consumption, and is said to be better off if he receives a more preferred bundle. There are two reasons for doubting if this is a satisfactory foundation for individualistic welfare economics. The first is empirical: it is doubtful if people are, always and everywhere, so purely selfish. The second is that it is hard to find much force in normative prescription for a world in which all agents are, by assumption, amoral. (The difficulty of a utilitarianism that accepts the axiom as descriptively accurate but goes on to recommend policy on utilitarian moral grounds is well known.) It therefore seems worth trying to relax this axiom if we can: we might gain in positive content *and* add moral force to normative individualistic prescription. We may indeed drop it, but we must enquire into the cost of doing so, and with what we may replace it.

Since Arrow (1951a), two outstanding contributions by Edgeworth (1881) have commonly been called the First and Second Theorems of Welfare Economics. The First Theorem is that any competitive equilibrium is a Pareto-optimum. The Second is that any optimal allocation can be supported by competitive prices if the initial endowment is appropriate.

There is no occasion to delay now to set out all the assumptions of the Edgeworth–Arrow theorems, some of which will be extensively discussed below. The immediate question is the effect that dropping the axiom of selfishness may have on these two theorems. The First Theorem is an obvious and immediate casuality. If economic agents are concerned with each other's welfare, there clearly may be competitive equilibrium, corresponding to some initial endowments, which are not optimal: they are not regarded as morally unacceptable merely by the outside observer, but by the agents themselves. So, can we "save" the Second Theorem? This is a very serious matter. We rely on this theorem for the notion that matters of equity and of efficiency may be considered separately, or "divorced." We rely on it for any notion that competition is efficient or "good" (at least in a strictly convex economy). Perhaps we rely on it overmuch, even in a convex economy, since it may be argued that deliberate or purposive redistribution cannot be lump-sum, that the idea is inherently self-contradictory (unless, perhaps, it can be based on observable but immutable individual characteristics). However this may be, the immediate question is what restrictions are required on preferences if they are to be extended (or interdependent) *and* it is still to be true that an optimum allocation can be supported by competitive prices (given, of course, the other necessary assumptions).

2.2 Edgeworth's treatment of extended preferences (1881)

This question has been investigated before – first, indeed, by Edgeworth (1881) himself! Edgeworth's work does not seem, however, to be very well known (it certainly has not reached the textbooks), and the subsequent history is rather diffuse. I therefore think it worthwhile to retell some of the story, using the opportunity to clarify some issues and correct some errors. Edgeworth considered the possibility of "sympathy" between economic agents. At one extreme, there is none: the neighbor's utility counts for nothing (the axiom of selfishness is satisfied). At the other extreme, the neighbor's utility "counts for one": it is as important to the agent's happiness as his own (the Purely Universalistic case, as Edgeworth called it). In between, the neighbor's utility will "count for a fraction." Edgeworth, as a utilitarian, was able to represent this, in the two-person two-good case, with the additively separable utility functions

$$U^A(x_A, y_A, x_B, y_B) = \alpha u^A(x_A, y_A) + (1-\alpha)u^B(x_B, y_B) \quad (2.1)$$
$$U^B(x_A, y_A, x_B, y_B) = \beta u^B(x_B, y_B) + (1-\beta)u^A(x_A, y_A) \quad (2.2)$$

with

$$0 \leq \alpha, \beta \leq 1$$

and, if we wish to draw a box, the constraints

$$x_A + x_B = x$$
$$y_A + y_B = y.$$

(I use here neither Edgeworth's notation nor that of Collard, 1975, although the latter very opportunely reminded us of Edgeworth's contribution.[2]) Here U^A and U^B are the individual's "grand utility functions": their arguments are all the elements of the complete allocation of all goods to all members of society. Since, in this formulation, their arguments are the private utilities of all agents (functions of their own private bundles), we may call U^A and U^B the individuals' social welfare functions. It does not seem empirically unreasonable to suppose that individuals are moral agents and have opinions about social welfare which may be represented in some such way. Before asking if there are "better," or less purely utilitarian, ways of representing the social preferences of individuals, it will be convenient to examine some properties of Edgeworth's representation.

First, as Edgeworth stated, it does not disturb or distort the contract curve we should obtain if we assumed the individuals to be, in fact, selfish, and drew the contract curve for the case $\alpha = \beta = 1$. To see this, assume that neither agent is entirely selfish, setting $0 < \alpha, \beta < 1$. Now, maximizing either of (2.1) or (2.2), subject to the other reaching some preassigned value

within the limits set by the quantity constraints, and rearrang-
ing the usual first-order conditions, we find the condition

$$u_1^A/u_2^A = u_1^B/u_2^B \tag{2.3}$$

(where the subscripts denote partial derivatives with respect to
the arguments by order). Here α and β have dropped out. We
have the same equal MRS condition that we normally obtain in
the selfish case, where $\alpha = \beta = 1$. Collard (1975) (and see his
1978) calls this the "no-twisting theorem." It is a remarkable
result. Before going on to investigate the second of Edgeworth's
claims (the "contraction" of the contract curve), we explore this
further.

We have the striking result that interdependent preferences,
in Edgeworth's representation, leave the contract curve – or at
least part of it, whence the Second Theorem of Welfare
Economics – undisturbed. How can this be?

Calculate, from (2.1), A's marginal rate of substitution
between goods in B's bundle. It is

$$\frac{U_3^A}{U_4^A} = \frac{(1-\alpha)u_1^B}{(1-\alpha)u_2^B} = \frac{u_1^B}{u_2^B} = \frac{U_3^B}{U_4^B}, \tag{2.4}$$

that is, A's MRS between goods in B's bundle *is* B's MRS (and
analogously, of course, for B's MRS between goods in A's
bundle). That is why, given the equity considerations represented by $0 < \alpha, \beta \le 1$, the Second Theorem holds. In the general,
benevolent, case of $\alpha, \beta < 1$, each of U^A, U^B is increasing in u^A and
u^B, which we may take to represent each individual's "enjoy-
ment" of his own consumption bundle. Yet the force of
Edgeworth's formulation is that each agent is concerned with
the other's wellbeing *only as that agent sees it*. Neither's concern for
the other's welfare induces him to try to interfere with the other's
choice of (private) consumption goods. This is what Donaldson
and I, in earlier work (Archibald and Donaldson, 1976a; 1976b;
1979) called the "non-paternalist condition." It seems to
represent J.S. Mill's (1859) rule that one may not seek to coerce
another individual for his own good, but only to avoid injury to
a third party. "Coercion" here would mean attempted interference with the other agent's choice of consumption bundle,

whether by direct interference with quantities or by selective use of prices (taxes or subsidies).[3] Clearly, if individuals' preferences are "sympathetic," in Edgeworth's sense, but do not satisfy the non-paternalist condition, then what these individuals may regard as an optimal allocation cannot, in general, be supported by competitive prices. This raises the issue, mentioned in section 1.1 above, of whether all, or any, preferences are to "count." I shall return to this question of restricted domain in section 2.7 below.

The second of Edgeworth's claims is that, although allowing $\alpha, \beta \neq 1$ does not distort or "twist" the contact curve, it may shorten the part of it that could be reached by voluntary exchange, what Edgeworth called the "pure" portion. Inspection of (2.1), or (2.2), suggests that there might be allocations such that, under constraint, A, or B, would disprefer a feasible change in his favor – that is, dU^A, under constraint, might become negative. Given diminishing first derivatives of the functions u^A, u^B (which Edgeworth certainly assumed), this at least seems possible. Consider the expression

$$dU^A = {}^a u_1^A dx_A + \alpha u_2^A dy_A + (1-\alpha)u_1^B(-dx_A) + (1-\alpha)u_2^B(-dy_A).$$
$$(2.5)$$

It is clearly possible that, under constraint, as 2.5 is written, dU^A may be zero or negative without any need for u_1^A or u_2^A to be negative (and analogously for dU^B).

At an allocation at which $(2.5) = 0$, we might say that A is "satisfied (socially) under constraint." If, similarly, B satiates at some positive, feasible allocation, then only intermediate allocations are optimal. In the neighborhood of such allocations – or, as we might say, "inside" the satiation points, if any exist in a box of given size – each individual is, and of course behaves as, an ordinary selfish maximizer. This case is illustrated in Figure 2.1. It is, of course, possible that both A and B are so benevolent that the set of such allocations is empty, but I shall neglect this case. (If the wounded soldier had in his turn insisted that Sir Phillip Sidney drink the water, we may wonder how they would have resolved the matter.) Collard (1975) draws the box diagram, and considers the possibility of "cross-over."

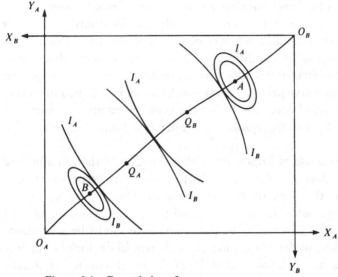

Figure 2.1 Extended preferences

Edgeworth thus offers a utilitarian representation of extended preferences that combine benevolence or "sympathy" with non-paternalism, and are consistent with the Second Theorem. The obvious question is whether or not this can be done without utilitarianism.

2.3 Winter's treatment (1969)

It was almost a century before this question was brilliantly answered by Winter (1969). I shall follow Winter's argument very closely (though with slight changes in notation). Let x_i be the ith consumer's consumption set, and X the entire set of all allocations of all goods to all consumers. Each consumer has a complete ordering of x_i given by $\underset{i}{\gtrsim}$ and of X given by $\underset{i}{\overset{\sigma}{\gtrsim}}$.

Consider two allocations X^0 and X' which differ only in that, in X', x_i^0 is replaced by x_i'. Winter imposes the following conditions on the orderings:

(1)   if $x_i' >_i x_i^0$ then $X' \overset{\sigma}{\underset{i}{>}} X^0$;

(2) $\quad x_i' \underset{i}{\gtrsim} x_1^0$ implies $X' \underset{k}{\overset{\sigma}{\gtrless}} X^0 \forall k.$ (2.6)

Condition (1) ensures that each agent always prefers an increase in his own bundle – or, in Edgeworth's terms, that $dU^A/du^A > 0$ as, without constraint, it must be. Condition (2) may be read "if i's new bundle is not dispreferred by i to his previous bundle, then the new allocation is not dispreferred by anyone." Thus Winter's conditions (2.6) impose simultaneously "sympathy," at least in the form of weak benevolence, *and* non-paternalism. That the Second Theorem holds is clear. An optimum relative to $\underset{i}{\overset{\sigma}{\gtrless}}$ must be an optimum relative to $\underset{i}{\gtrsim}$ by (2.6), whence, given the other necessary assumptions, it can be supported by a price system (see Debreu, 1959, and Winter for further detail). Winter goes on to remark that each consumer's preferences over X might be of the form of a Bergson social welfare function, $W^i(u^i(x_i), \ldots, u^m(x_m))$. We may say that, if the functions W^i are monotonically increasing in all arguments we have strict benevolence, whereas if it is required only that W^i be monotonically increasing in u^i and non-decreasing in all its other arguments, we have weak benevolence, allowing a wider class of social preference. Winter points out "that there is more scope for reliance upon the price mechanism in a community of men of good will than in a community of men of ill will – provided that the good will is accompanied by respect for each other's tastes" (1969, p. 101). It is, of course, true that good will, or benevolence, as defined by Winter, Rader (1980),[4] and Lemche (1986a; 1986b), implies or includes the non-paternalist condition. It may be, however, as we shall see, useful to separate them.

2.4 Archibald and Donaldson's treatment (1976a)

What Donaldson and I tried to do was "unpack" Winter's condition (2.6) on preferences so that non-paternalism and "sympathy" (preferences on distribution) might be separated, and so that we could give a functional representation to preferences, and employ standard calculus methods, without having to follow Edgeworth's utilitarianism. Unfortunately, in our (1976a) at least, we made a mistake. I shall take this opportunity of setting out what we did and correcting our mistake.

Instead of Edgeworth's (2.1) and (2.2), we write the preferences of the ith agent in the weakly separable form as

$$U^i(X) = \phi^i[h^i(x_1^1, \ldots, x_n^1), h^2(x_1^2, \ldots, x_n^2), \ldots,$$
$$h^i(x_i^i, \ldots, x_n^i), \ldots, h^m(x_1^m, \ldots, x_n^m)] \qquad (2.7)$$

(in an obvious notation for a n-good m-agent society). (2.7) clearly represents preferences that satisfy the non-paternalist condition and, assuming $\phi_j^i \geq 0 \, \forall i, j$, at least Winter's weak benevolence. Thus i's MRS between two goods, r and s, say, in j's bundle is given by

$$\frac{\dfrac{\partial U^i}{\partial x_r^j}}{\dfrac{\partial U^i}{\partial x_s^j}} = \frac{\phi_j^i h_r^j}{\phi_j^i h_s^j} = \frac{h_r^j}{h_s^j}. \qquad (2.8)$$

Agent i thus "respects" agent j's MRS. We might replace the functions $h^i(\cdot)$ in (2.7) by Edgeworth's $u^i(\cdot)$ but need not, since the functions $h^j(\cdot)$ need not, of course, be cardinal indicators of j's wellbeing. Any monotonic increasing transform of a function representing j's ordering will clearly serve, but even this is not necessary. Any agent who does not seek to interfere with another's choice, and is at least weakly benevolent towards him, will be content that he, and all others, are free to enjoy the gains from trade. Thus not only will the Second Theorem hold, but we do not have to presume agents to be ridiculously well informed about each other's preferences: if the initial endowment is acceptable, so too is the competitive allocation.

Weak separability thus captures Mill's principle of non-paternalism without the additive separability of Edgeworth. The trouble came over the signs of the partial derivatives of the ϕ^i. Donaldson and I did not want to insist on Winter's condition of weak benevolence, which becomes here $\phi_j^i \geq 0 \, \forall X$ and $\forall j$. We wanted to allow, that is, the possibility that $\phi_j^i < 0$ for some i and j at some X. This was not to capture any notion of "malevolence" (presumably if i were truly malevolent towards j, we should have $\phi^i_j < 0\ \forall X$). Our object was to capture some possibly appealing moral views.

(1) Suppose that world GNP increases by \$1 mn., and that every cent of it goes to some ostentatious and vulgar millionaire (or sadistic dictator, or drug baron, or what you will). Would it not be nice to be able to say stoutly "the world is worse off," instead of, relatively tamely, "the world *could* have been better off, but cannot be worse off"?

(2) In the same way, are there not allocations of which one might like to say simply "j has too much"?

(3) The moral rule of "reversibility" requires, however, that if one is willing to say that, at some X, j has too much, then at some X one would have to admit that one has oneself too much: $\phi^i_i < 0$, some X.

As we may see, the possibility that some ϕ^i_j (including possibly $j = i$) be non-positive at some X cannot be admitted if the Second Theorem is to be saved (although it is possible to represent most of the distributional (moral) views that Donaldson and I wished to).

(a) If we adopt Bliss' "nested set" definition of separability, then partial derivatives of a separable function ϕ^i cannot switch signs (see Blackorby, Primont, and Russell, 1978).

(b) Lemche (1986b) reasonably asked, what is i to do if, at some X, $\phi^i_i < 0$ while h^i is still an increasing function? What is i to maximize? (We had made no provision for satiation of the $h^i(\cdot)$ and I do not intend to.)

If only to avoid this dilemma, we must assume $\phi^i_i > 0, \forall i, \forall X$. Then the moral rule of reversability, if nothing else, requires $\phi^i_j > 0\ \forall i, j\ \forall X$. Thus rather than accepting Winter's restriction of weak benevolence, here $\phi^i_j \geq 0, \forall X, \forall j$ (as Donaldson and I did in our 1976b and 1979). I shall henceforth assume that these derivatives are all strictly positive. We can, nonetheless, represent most of the possible moral views of distribution that we sought to capture in the first place. What we have to accept, of course, is that the functions ϕ^i represent *orderings*. i may rank an increase in j's allocation or wellbeing as low as he likes relative to that of others; but if we have only ordinal rankings, we cannot insist on there being a zero, and negative numbers.

What makes it possible, nonetheless, to represent certain interesting distributional preferences is what we may call the GNP constraint. Thus consider the expression

$$dU^i = \phi^i_j \nabla h^j \mathbf{dx} + \phi^i_k \nabla h^k(-\mathbf{dx}) \tag{2.9}$$

(in a standard notation). dU^i may, of course, be positive, negative, or zero, at some X, without any requirement that any partial derivative of ϕ^i be negative or that any $h^i(\cdot)$ be non-increasing. We can thus both drop cardinality and impose strong benevolence without losing our ability to represent the preferences of an agent who prefers, disprefers, or is indifferent to a transfer between j and k. Indeed, we can still represent the preferences of an agent i who, at some X, prefers a transfer from himself to some other agent.

We have here the "ordinal analogy" to the model of Edgeworth that led to (2.5) above; and, indeed, Figure 2.1 will still serve to illustrate a possible case. We can also still capture most of the force of the distributional views that Donaldson and I wished to represent. (1) cannot be recaptured in its stoutest form, but one may still say "At this X, giving this windfall to that k is the least beneficial thing that could have been done with it." (2) has to be more carefully worded, but one may still say "At this X, a transfer from j to k would be preferred." The rule of reversibility then requires (3) "At some X, a transfer from myself to k would be good," which is, from (2.9), consistent with our assumptions.

It is here that we see the convenience of distinguishing between benevolence and non-paternalism. Suppose that, at some X, (2.9) or its analogy is positive for some i,j,k. Thus agent i might prefer a transfer from some j to some k. No malevolence towards j is implied (at least, if i would prefer a transfer in the other direction at some other X, perhaps the mirror-image of this one). Furthermore, if i is non-paternalist (benevolent), he will wish the transfer to be effected in the least distorting manner possible (by lump-sum methods if they are feasible). Thus, even an egalitarian, if he is a non-paternalist, might be uneasy about effecting the transfer by, say, excise taxes on "luxury" consumer goods and housing subsidies or food stamps, at least if he thinks a less distorting method (Mill's inheritance taxes, perhaps) to be feasible.

(I venture to offer the reader a simple test of the empirical relevance of (2.9) and the accompanying argument. Let us agree that his own $h^i(\cdot)$ is a strictly increasing function. Under the GNP constraint, would he prefer an increase in his own allocation, x^i, irrespective of from whom the transfer was made? If the answer is "no," he cannot satisfy the axiom of selfishness; and he must think that there are some members of society who, at the given X, are getting "not more than enough.")

2.5 Lemche's treatment (1986a)

Even if we accept the restriction $\phi^i_j > 0$, (2.7) has another implication which we may notice. The separable form requires not merely that each agent respects others' preferences, but that he "respects his own": since $h^i(\cdot)$ contains no argument from the consumption bundle of any other, all Veblen effects – snob and bandwagon – are excluded (as, indeed, was pointed out in Archibald and Donaldson, 1976a). The axiom of selfishness, as normally interpreted, excludes them too (but see Leibenstein, 1950). Nonetheless, this restriction may be unwelcome on empirical grounds. Lemche (1986a) shows that benevolence and non-paternalism may be represented more generally, and without this particular restriction (which follows also from Winter's definition). To do this, he introduces what he calls *conditional preferences*.

Let the allocation be $X = (X_1, \ldots, X_i, \ldots, X_m)$ (in a slight change from Lemche's notation: otherwise, I follow him very closely), let $X^{-1} = (X_1, \ldots, X_{i-1}, X_{i+1}, \ldots, X_m)$, and for any $\hat{X}_i$ let $(\hat{X}_i; X^{-i}) = (X_i, \ldots, X_{i-1}, \hat{X}_i, X_{i+1}, \ldots, X_m)$. Now $(\hat{X}_i; X^{-i})$ is the allocation X with $\hat{X}_i$ substituted for X_i, and $\phi^i(\hat{X}_i; X^{-i})$ is the value of ϕ_i at this allocation. The ith agent's *conditional preferences* for the jth agent's consumption given X^{-j} are represented by $\phi^i(X_j; X^{-j})$, for constant X^{-j} (for which we may write $\phi^i(X_j | X^{-j})$). Thus $\phi^i(X_j | X^{-j})$ expresses i's ranking of alternative consumption bundles for agent j given X^{-j}. It is induced by – or, we may say, "drawn from" – i's ordering of the complete allocations X, $\phi^i(X)$, but for a constant X^{-j}. If it is independent of $X^{-j} \forall j$ (including i), then $\phi^i(X)$ and $\phi^i(X_i | X^{-i})$ is the $h^i(X_i)$ defined above.

We may now define non-paternalism. Agent i is a non-paternalist if and only if

$$\phi^j(\hat{X}_j | X^{-j}) = \phi^j(\mathring{X}_j | X^{-j}) \Rightarrow \phi^i(\hat{X}_j | X^{-j}) = \phi^i(\mathring{X}_j | X^{-j}),$$
(2.10)

$\forall_j$, X, and $\hat{X}_j, \mathring{X}_j$

2.6   The Second Theorem and public goods

We see, then, that the Second Theorem survives if we drop the axiom of selfishness provided that we impose the restriction of non-paternalism on extended preferences, given that all goods are private. We now introduce public goods (as was first done by Lemche, 1986b, in the case of extended preferences), and ask if the same, or any analogous, restriction can be maintained, or is useful. (I do not intend to discuss public goods elsewhere in this book, whence this section may be regarded as a digression, and skipped. I, however, think it is worthwhile to complete the present discussion of extended preferences.)

Recall the form of (2.7) above, and consider

$$V^i(X,z) = \phi^i[g^1(x^1, z^1), \ldots, g^i(x^i, z^i), \ldots, g^m(x^m, z^m)] \quad (2.11)$$

where the x^i are vectors of private goods, as are the z^i of pure public goods. The definition of "publicness" implies, of course the technological constraint $z^i = z, \forall_i$. The form of (2.11) implies that agent i "respects" every other individual's MRS between an element of his own private allocation (x^j, say) and z. Lemche (1986a) shows that, in the case of pure public goods, this condition actually requires that preferences are "the same" (up to some monotonic transform) if the equilibrium of the allocation mechanism is competitive in the sense that the MRS between each pair of goods is the same for all agents. Relying on the fact that benevolence, as defined by Winter and himself, implies non-paternalism, Lemche writes only of "benevolence." His proof is more general than that given below, in that he does not reply on a specific functional form ((2.11) here), but less general in that he confines himself to the case of two consumers, two private goods, and one public good. The generalization to many dimensions is largely a matter of notation and rather tedious arithmetic: the insight is his.

Let us write $\text{MRS}^i(x_r^i, z_s)$ for agent i's MRS between a good (say, x_r^i) in his private consumption bundle and a public good (z_s, say). The non-paternalist condition requires that this be equal to $\text{MRS}^j(x_r^i, z_s)$ in an obvious extension of the notation. Similarly, it is required that $\text{MRS}^i(x_k^j, z_s) = \text{MRS}^j(x_k^j, z_s)$. We may evaluate one of these terms:

$$\text{MRS}^i(x_r^i, z_s) = \frac{\phi_i^i g_r^i}{\sum_q \phi_q^i g_s^q}. \tag{2.12}$$

The only surprise here is the denominator, where $\Sigma(\cdot\ \cdot)$ denotes the sum of the partial derivatives of i's social welfare function $V^i(X, z)$, each weighted by the appropriate derivative g_s^q, where q ranges over the whole population. It is the nature of a public good, in combination with the non-paternalism condition, that i cannot be selective here: the denominator of (2.13) cannot be limited to $\phi_{i}^j g_s^i$, nor when we consider $\text{MRS}^j(x_r^i, z_s)$ can the denominator be limited to $\phi_j^j g_s^j$. If we evaluate all four terms in this manner, take advantage of common denominators ($\Sigma q \phi_q^i g_s^q$ and $\Sigma q \phi_q^j q_s^q$), and rearrange, we find that

$$\phi_i^i / \phi_j^i = \phi_i^j / \phi_j^j \tag{2.13}$$

which may be further rearranged at will. What it amounts to is that each individual's weighting of his own welfare relative to that of another's must be the same as the other's. This is clearly "too much": it is more than is intended by the assumption of benevolence, but it is the consequence of that condition in combination with the (definitional) technology of a public good.

If all goods are strictly private, extended preferences may be represented by (2.7) above, with the restrictions of non-paternalism and benevolence imposed. In this case, each agent is content that others enjoy the gains from trade, making their utility-maximizing choices of their own private consumption bundles. An optimum allocation may thus be supported by competitive prices. It is in this sense that we may speak of agents "respecting" each others' tastes, conveniently summarized by their MRSs: they do not have to know them. In the case of public goods, this condition of non-paternalism, or "respect," has no sensible interpretation. An agent may refrain from seeking to interfere in another's choice between bread and beer, but another's choice between private and public goods, or among public goods, is a choice *for* both of them. Thus, in the presence of public goods, there is no analogy to non-paternalism. An agent cannot simultaneously "respect" his own preferences between bread and beer and submarines and schools, and the (different) preferences of another. He must respect his own (or resign).

The conclusion of ch. 2 is that the Second Theorem survives the introduction of extended preferences if we are willing to follow Edgeworth in imposing the restrictions of benevolence and non-paternalism (although we need not adopt his linearly separable form). The non-paternalist restriction is, however, of no help in dealing with public goods. Pursuit of this problem leads immediately to Arrow's general problem of social choice, which is entirely beyond the scope of this book.

2.7   Non-paternalism

One question still to consider, albeit briefly, is whether there is any justification in imposing the non-paternalist condition. It is certainly convenient: *if*, empirically, extended preferences are important (on which I shall present no evidence), then it appears to be the only way to preserve any case for free markets or *laissez faire*. Whether it is empirically justified is another matter. It may be morally justified: it appears, as I have suggested, to follow from J.S. Mill's *Essay on Liberty* (1859). His justification is, however, not without difficulty. In the first place, the arguments of the *Essay* are all ostensibly derived from a strictly utilitarian foundation (with no reliance on "rights'" arguments), and we are not all utilitarians. In the second place, it has been doubted if Mill's conclusions do follow satisfactorily from utilitarian foundations. (For vehement disagreement by an approximately contemporary utilitarian, see Stephen, 1874. For modern doubts, see Brown, 1972 and 1973, and Ten, 1980.)

Donaldson and I (1976b) tried to base a defense on the "negative version of the Golden Rule: do not do unto others as you would not be done to" (see Baier, 1958). This seemed attractive: "if you do not agree to others interfering in your private choice, do not attempt to interfere with the choices of others." Unfortunately, the "negative version" lacks force, since ethical rules derived from it depend on each individual's tastes (or quirks), whence it can be made consistent with many rules. I must leave the matter there.

One might, nonetheless, be tempted to judge that only non-paternalist preferences over private goods should "count": it is possible that such a restriction on the domain would ease some of the difficulties of the theory of social choice. I have not investigated the matter, but cannot in fact be optimistic: it is precisely when we introduce public goods that we need a theory of social choice, since here we cannot appeal to the Second Theorem, and it is precisely here that the non-paternalist condition fails us.

2.8 Envy

There remain two other attempts to extend the scope of welfare economics to include distributional considerations which must be briefly noted. The first depends on envy. Agent i is said to envy agent j if

$$u^i(x^j) > u^i(x^i).$$

An allocation at which there is no envy is said to be equitable. If it is also efficient, it is said to be fair. (See Varian, 1974; 1975; 1976.) When it was shown that a fair allocation could at least be achieved by equal initial endowments, it seemed that a rabbit had indeed come out of a hat: a case for egalitarianism among agents themselves satisfying the axiom of selfishness, to whom it was not necessary to attribute any distributional preferences, and which required of the observer, or adviser, only the judgements that envy is "bad" and efficiency "good." It was then shown by Pazner and Schmeidler (1978) that, in a production economy, a fair allocation may not exist. An attempt to restore the situation was made by an appeal to "productivity ethics." Here, an agent is not "allowed" to envy another's bundle if he could, by working hard enough, enjoy the same bundle. This amounts to the arbitrary exclusion of leisure from the utility function, or least from preferences that are to "count." These points were made in Archibald and Donaldson (1979). Baumol (1986) then published his book *Superfairness*, the title of which is so misleading: the book should be called *The Economics of Superselfishness*. Baumol's agents are quite amoral: they not only satisfy the axiom of selfishness but are willing to agree to some restrictions on their choice (e.g. wartime rationing) merely to insure themselves against the envy that would be aroused if others were to get more. I can only wonder why anyone should care about equity in such a moral rats' nest, and leave the subject, save for one last point.

An attempt has been made to "endogenize" envy – that is, to write utility functions that represent it, as they properly should. Sussangkarn and Goldman (1983) suggest three functional forms, and show that, in general, such functions are inconsistent with the existence of fair (equitable and efficient) allocations. To take only one example, i's utility function may be written as $T^i[u^i(x^i),(u^i(x^i)-u^i(x^j))],i\neq j,T^i$ real valued and strictly monotonic. After our discussion of non-paternalism, the appearance of x^j as an argument of T^i in this form suggests danger. Separability has gone. Agent i is interested not just in j's income, or in some index of his wellbeing, but in his actual, physical, consumption bundle. He may just envy j's larger bundle, but he may specifically grudge j his consumption of champagne (or beer). He may now be happier if j cannot buy champagne at the same competitive price that he can himself. We cannot expect the Second Theorem to survive the introduction of preferences of this sort, but we may well think that, if envy is to be taken more seriously, it should be treated in the manner of Sussang-karn and Goldman.

2.9   "Models of the dog and his master"

I must finally mention accounts of what has been called Pareto-optimal redistribution. Donaldson and I discussed them (1976a) under the heading "Models of the Dog and his Master," and I need only summarize what we said there. In these models, the Master is represented as the "Representative Rich Man" and the Dog as the "Representative Poor Man." Their utility functions are asymmetric. The Dog's welfare appears as an argument of his Master's utility function, but not vice versa. Clearly, it may amuse the Master to throw some bones to the Dog, whose role is solely to enjoy them: he is not permitted to question the justice of the original distribution. This is called "Optimal Redistribution." The obvious implication is that we, no more than the Dog, are to question the original distribution. Suppose, however, that the endowments were changed. Then, if the utility functions were not swapped too, we should have a wealthy and entirely selfish Dog, and a poor Master who would still have concern for the Dog's welfare. There would be no redistribution (from Rich to Poor, at least) and this would be "optimal." I suppose that this might be an empirically plausible description of some inequitable but stable society. The line of argument can obviously be extended. The Rich might think it judicious to throw some bones to the Dogs: "don't grind the faces of the poor too hard, or they may break your windows." There is ample historical precedent for this sort of prudential transfer (protection money?): "bread and circuses." One might, however, feel a little squeamish about calling it, in any sense, "optimal."

Part II

Iterative controls

3

Feed-back control processes

3.1 Iterative controls in real time

In this chapter, I discuss the use of iterative feed-back systems for economic control. Their appealing feature is that they combine into one process several steps in economic planning: data gathering, computation, *and* implementation. One drawback is obvious: they operate in real time, with whatever costs are consequent upon quantities (prices) being "wrong" during the process itself. A second drawback is less obvious, but will emerge as we consider examples (e.g. section 5.7 below). The most these processes can do is enforce, at the partial equilibrium level, qualitative rules or targets derived (although not quantitatively computed) from general equilibrium welfare theory. In their present form, at least, it is not clear how to adapt them in cases in which rules derived from general welfare theory are in some way wrong or inadequate. I can only point out the difficulties here, and leave it to the reader to judge whether real-time feed-back systems, as a method of control alternative to economic planning, deserve further consideration.

Not all the control mechanisms described in this book in fact rely on adaptive systems; those that do not are reserved to Part IV. It is required of them, too, that they economize on information and computation, and that, by providing suitable incentives, economize also on policemen.

3.2 The Criterion Function

It is thought that many organisms operate partially, or even entirely, as simple feed-back control processes. (See papers in

Day and Groves, 1975.) It has been suggested that human-controlled institutions may operate in much the same way. Thus the business firm, prevented by ignorance and computational difficulty from *calculating* the profit-maximizing output may use a simple hill-climbing technique to reach the neighborhood of the profit-maximizing output. (For the view that profit-seeking firms cannot *calculate* profit-maximizing levels of output – or anything else – see Nelson and Winter, 1982, and, of course, the work of Herbert Simon cited therein. For models of a firm using a simple feed-back hill-climbing technique, "driving by the rear-vision mirror," see Day, 1967 and Day and Tinney, 1968. For further discussion, see again Day and Groves, 1975.) Applications of feed-back methods to deliberate, humanly-engineered, control processes, are commonplace: thermostats, automatic pilots, and the like. Here I shall suggest the deliberate application of these techniques to economic control as an alternative to planning. There is, however, a crucial distinction between the familiar use of feed-back systems for physical control and their potential use for economic control: in the former use, the target must be set, i.e. pre-selected; in the latter use, the target must somehow "emerge" as the process goes on. If this were not the case, we should at the most have a system for the implementation of a plan, not a substitute for the planning process itself. If, that is, the target value had, like an oven temperature, to be pre-selected, the information and computational requirements of planning would still be required.

To say that a target value must somehow "emerge" is very vague. What is required, as part of the control process, is selection of an index or *Criterion Function*, easily observable during the process, and with the property that success – or at least improvement – is indicated by it. Thus, though the object is generally an increase in welfare, or the achievement of some goal thought to be associated with efficiency, the Criterion Function need not necessarily be a welfare index: it may be a surrogate. It is difficult, at this stage of the argument, to give examples. One (see ch. 4) is the sum of total profit in two competitive industries, one of which incurs costs consequent upon the activity of the other (the simple producer–producer externality case). Other examples will be presented below. The difficulty is better admitted now: I see no way of generalizing further – of saying, that is, more than that in each case in which a feed-back control is proposed, *a* Criterion Function must be *found*; and that it must have two properties: that its behavior is easily known from information automatically generated during the process, and that it gives a clear signal – e.g. by changing direction – when we are at (or at least in a neighborhood of) our target.

The disadvantages of a control process are, of course, due to the fact that the search procedure takes place in actual, or market, time rather than in planning time. It therefore requires that the environment be stable relative to the speed of convergence of the search procedures. It is also subject to the usual difficulties over income effects. If, contrary to what is now assumed, there are indivisibilities and irreversibilities in the technology, and, in particular, the process is slow relative to the stability of the environment (see section 4.5 below), then serious losses during the process are possible. In fact, a major difficulty is simply that of knowing whether one has a suitable case for the application of so simple a process. Nonetheless, it seems worth trying to follow the advice of Day (1975, p. 28): "Policy-oriented research in this field [adaptive control] should aim at identifying control mechanisms of an adaptive nature that can improve economic performance, primarily from the point of view of viability (homeostasis) and secondarily from the point of view of efficiency." Rosen (1975, p. 40) added to this "it [adaptive control] is at the centre of the technologies we require to control our own human institutions, especially in the economic and political realm."

3.3 Requirements of a planning and of a control process

We note first some well known requirements of economic planning:

1 There must be some qualitative rule to determine what is optimal or at least "desirable."
2 Information must be collected at the planning centre,

which in turn may require some incentives for truth revelation.

3 A *planning process* must put together 1 and 2 to compute a numerical solution.

4 There must exist some system of implementation, usually entailing an incentive structure (rewards and punishments) to translate the solutions of 3 into action.

To this list, Malinvaud (1967) (see also Heal, 1973), as is well known, has added some desirable properties of 3:

3.1 Feasibility at each step.
3.2 Convergence.
3.3 Monotonicity.

These three together ensure that, wherever the process may be truncated, the solution will be "better" – a step in the right direction.

We may now draw up a parallel list for an iterative, or adaptive, control process:

1A The same.

2A.1 The need for data collection by the centre is eliminated, *but* sufficient step-by-step information to check against the Criterion Function must be easily ascertainable at every step in the process.

2A.2 We thus require what I have called above a *Criterion Function*: some index, consistent with 1 or 1A, which tells us whether we are going in the right direction, or perhaps overshooting.

3A There is no need for anyone to compute optimal or target values – no need, that is, for a planning process as such, but an *iterative control process* must be designed, which should, indeed, display the properties listed as desirable by Malinvaud, and more.

3A.1 Feasibility is built into a real-time iterative control process unless the control has the wholly undesirable property that, at some parameter values, solutions are "off the map" (zero, infinite, or otherwise unattainable).

3A.2 Convergence has to be established, as for any process.

3A.3 Monotonicity is obviously desirable, but there may prove to be a trade-off between monotonicity (at least in the neighborhood of equilibrium) and another obviously desirable property, that the control be *strategy-proof* (see particularly section 5.5 below).

4A A system for implementation is not now a separate requirement: a feed-back control system *is* an implementation system. We may recall the example of a thermostat (and that what distinguishes an economic control is the manner in which the target value is found). An economic control depends, however, on implementation by human agents, so we may note more desirable properties here:

4A.1 Incentive compatibility at each step.

4A.2 Proof against strategic behavior.

4A.2 may be thought to be implied by 4A.1 but, as we shall see, it requires special attention.

3.4 Other properties of control processes

Some further comments on 4A seem called for. The substitution of control processes for planning permits "decentralization" in several senses. The first is informational: no agent has to report, or reveal, preferences or production possibilities to any authority, except in so far as these are revealed by his observable actions (we might say "easily observable": such magnitudes as price, quantity, or profit). A second is computational: *no one* has to – or could – *compute* target values. A third relates to implementation. A control process has the implementation stage of a plan built into it. It follows that it must be in the interests of individual agents to move in the desired direction at each step. This property is required. It follows, however, that there is no need to write "truth revelation" as a separate desirable property. If the process is incentive-compatible at each step, individual actions will reveal all that needs to be known (the "truth") at each step.

It may be easy to show that a particular process is incentive-compatible at each step for myopic agents. We also need to ensure that longer-sighted agents, discerning the direction in which the process is taking them, do not find it in their own interest, at the sacrifice of some immediate benefit, to act in such a way as to slow down the convergence of the process, or even to block it completely. In at least some cases (see ch. 5), this may be ensured against by the introduction to the process of an arbitrary rule about parameter adjustment, at the price of losing speed in convergence and possibly monotonicity, at least in the neighborhood of equilibrium.

If we have the criterion function required in 2A.2, and the control is strategy-proof, then we have a *stopping rule*: the process terminates at, or close to, the target value indicated by (for example) an extreme value of the Criterion Function. This suggests some further necessary or desirable properties which may conveniently be listed under 4A.

4A.3   Since a real-time control process is necessarily *discrete* we cannot hope to converge precisely to any target value, but only to some neighborhood of it. We must thus select a *satisficing parameter* to supplement the stopping rule – stopping the process, that is, when the last parameter change has provoked a change in the observed value of the Criterion Function no larger than the satisficing parameter. Once again, there may be a trade-off between desirable properties of a control. On the one hand, the smaller the satisficing parameter may be, the better: we may come the closer to a target value. On the other hand, the real world is never free of disturbance, and too fine a setting – too little "tolerance" – might well cause the control to "hunt" in a most unsatisfactory manner. Yet again, it must not be set with so much tolerance that the control does not respond to changes in the parameters of the system being controlled. I know, unfortunately, no general *a priori* rules for the choice of satisficing parameters. Some might well be derived by the use of such devices as loss functions, but I do not pursue the matter. There is one more desirable property to note.

4A.4 The process must converge "reasonably" fast relative to the (in)stability of its environment. Obviously much the same may be said of the choice of planning period and the calendar duration of "planning time." There are, perhaps, two points worth noticing here. The first is that the use of improved hill-climbing techniques (e.g. second-order terms) may speed up a process only at the risk of making it prone to strategic behavior (see ch. 5). The second is more general. *Any* control process is limited by the speed with which the economic agents involved react to (deliberate) changes in *their* environment. If their reaction is sluggish, no control can be better than sluggish. I return to this point in section 3.5 below.

3.5 Decentralization

In section 3.4 above, it was argued that the control processes under discussion are informationally decentralized in certain senses. They are also decentralized in quite another way, for which there does not seem to be a convenient term. We may say that they are insensitive, or invariant to, resource ownership. If, say, an industry is to be controlled by the methods proposed here, it does not matter who may own the equity. Thus, as will become evident in the example to be given in ch. 4, these methods do not presuppose public ownership of the means of production. They are equally applicable in cases of private ownership which include, as I hope to show later, the limiting case of cooperative ownership by workers. Who may own the share certificates is immaterial. What is material is motivation.

I shall assume, except when otherwise noted, that the motive of consumers is always utility maximization, and that that of the managers of firms is profit maximization in the case of capitalist ownership, or the maximization of a reward function set as part of the control in the case of public ownership. (Cooperative ownership is differently dealt with: see Part IV below.) If managers are slow to maximize, or just not very good at it, the speed of any control process is limited. If their object is otherwise, as has often thought to be possible or even probable in insufficiently competitive environments, it would be necessary to know that objective in order to design an appropriate control. I shall not consider such cases here. It would, however, be inconsistent to argue, or at least to imply, that the requirements of central planning (in information, computation, and implementation) are such that it is desirable to look for easier alternatives, yet assume that managers solve the analogous problem immediately and costlessly. Even in a "fairly competitive" capitalist environment they may, indeed, do little more themselves than drive by the rear-vision mirror! In ch. 4 I deliberately consider a case in which they do just that, and consider methods to speed up the control process.

Nelson and Winter (1982) draw together arguments which now have a considerable history to show why firms may not be very good at profit-maximizing, and consider formally how they may proceed to search for greater profit, which is to say that the assumption that profit is the object is not dropped. The argument here is intended to be, as far as possible, consistent with that of Nelson and Winter. We may hope that, in an environment which is competitive in some long-run sense, the firms that survive are those that have learned to adapt reasonably quickly to changes in their environment. That would facilitate the sort of control process considered in ch. 4. It is not easy to think of any analogous process of natural selection for firms in public ownership. The managerial reward structures to be considered depend for their efficacy entirely on the rational greed of managers. If this is not a sufficient incentive, we have major trouble!

3.6 Phillips' controls

The reference to controls such as automatic pilots – servomechanisms – in section 3.2 may have reminded the reader of the exciting work of the late Bill Phillips. In his classic study on stabilization policy (1957) Phillips taught us all the principles of design of the automatic macro-pilot for an economy with lagged responses. The difficulty, as is well known, is that Phillips' control mechanism took no account of the possible response of self-interested agents to the controls, or to the control mechanism itself. Critical reaction to Phillips' work was perhaps an influence in the movement to study the "micro-foundations of macro-theory." Certainly the rational expectations model, at least in extreme form, offers an approach completely antithetical to that of Phillips. There is indeed something inherently contradictory about Phillips' controls. Implementation requires that the parameters of the system to be controlled be estimated. The estimation of the pre-control system will take some control parameters – such as government expenditures, tax rates, and the rate of interest – as exogenous. The installation of the control makes them endogenous, and itself requires re-estimation (of a system which is presumably now under-identified). Phillips was himself well aware of this problem, but devoted his attention to estimation methods rather than to individual behavior. Much the same criticisms can be made, *mutatis mutandis*, of the work of Theil on decision rules for government (see particularly his 1964).

I hope that it will be transparent that in this work I am not concerned with adaptive control in Phillips' sense, and that not merely because I am concerned with the control of firms and industries rather than with macro-control. The directional inertia of a ship is, after all, a constant, quite independent of what agency controls the rudder, and no component of the mechanism to be controlled can sensibly be thought to have any self-interest or expectations. The self-interested behavior of the agents to be controlled is here the centre of concern.

The very word "agents" in the last sentence must suggest that the partial-equilibrium control of managers (of individual firms or industries) is, in some sense, a principal–agent problem. So, of course, it is. My reasons for not dealing with it formally and explicitly as such are given in section 5.1 below. One must also be reminded of the extensive literature on "regulation," surveyed by Besanko and Sappington (1987). Discussion of this is postponed to section 5.2. Thus my order of argument is to give, in ch. 4, a very simple (indeed, stylized) example of a feed-back iterative control process at work, and then, in ch. 5, to consider its relationship to some other recent literature.

4

First example: an externality problem[1]

4.1 Information requirements

In ch. 4, I describe the application of a real-time iterative control process to the control of a producer–producer externality. The example is very simple. It may, however, serve several purposes here. First, it provides an opportunity to display in some detail the mechanics of such a process, which may be unfamiliar to some readers. Second, it allows us to check the process against the list of necessary or desirable properties given in section 3.3 above. Third – and perhaps most important – it provides an opportunity to state and consider some necessary, and restrictive, technological assumptions. Consideration of strategic behavior is deferred to ch. 5. Ch. 4 concludes with some brief remarks on the relationship between the control problem studied here and the more general problem of Second Best.

It may be helpful to explain at the beginning who "we" are. "We" are government or some agency thereof, perhaps a Ministry of Production. We might even be the members of the Planning Commission for some industry or group of industries who have decided that the best way to discharge their office is to make it redundant. We are, in any event, in charge of designing the control process.

While methods of deriving optimal tax functions to control producer–producer externalities, at least in simple cases, are very well known, the computation of *rates* has remained a difficult problem. It seems that we must have enough information to evaluate one or more partial derivatives at the optimal values of their arguments. This would require that we had sufficient information to solve the primal planning problem itself! The matter is not in fact so difficult. Groves and Loeb (1975) proposed a planning algorithm for determining the optimal supply of a public good used as an input by a group of firms. Groves (1976) adapted this algorithm to the producer–producer externality problem, requiring only that the parties to the externality (polluter, pollutees) knew and honestly reported their profit functions to the central authority. Taking advantage of the well known fact that, on certain quite reasonable assumptions, maximization of joint profit (merger) involves setting the externality at its optimal level, Groves pointed out that the central authority, knowing the profit functions, could then directly compute that level, without having to know the optimal level of anything else. He then ingeniously solved the problem of constructing an incentive structure such that it would pay the firms to report their profit functions honestly.

That firms do actually know their profit *functions* may be thought a rather strong assumption. Here, I shall relax that assumption. A scheme of search for the optimal tax is suggested which, like Groves', takes advantage of joint maximization, but requires only that firms, searching for profit, know and honestly report realized profit in each period. I shall in fact make the somewhat extreme assumption that firms have only a working knowledge of their immediate environment, including the savings and costs associated with current pollution levels. They can thus respond to small parameter changes with purposeful local searches, but cannot reveal information that they do not have. It will quickly be apparent that what matters is that they do maximize, as does the speed at which they do it, whereas their actual method matters not at all, except in so far as they do not possess the information which would allow us, if we had it, to proceed directly to the optimal solution.

In section 3.5 above, I suggested that the structure of property ownership might be irrelevant to the use of control processes, provided that the motivation of the agents was purposeful and well understood. In this chapter, it is assumed that the firms are privately owned profit maximizers (although perhaps not very well informed). In ch. 5, it is assumed that the firms are publicly owned, and that each has some monopoly power. It is natural to ask how the control process described in this chapter would have to be modified if the firms, although competitive, were publicly owned. There is a simple answer, which I think will become evident as the discussion progresses. Since they are, by assumption, operating in perfect competition, all that is necessary is to ensure that they do attempt profit maximizations, perhaps by making the managers' rewards depend on the profits.

4.2 The example: an upstream–downstream externality

In this example, we have the simplest case of an upstream–downstream externality. The upstream industry discharges pollution, z, as a byproduct of its production process, which imposes costs on the downstream industry. It is proposed to regulate this pollution by use of a specific tax at rate t. To set an optimal tax t^* on pollution, or directly to set an optimal pollution level z^*, without solving the primal planning problem, it is necessary to find an appropriate Criterion Function which reaches its maximum (or minimum) precisely at t^*, z^*. Groves (1976) takes as criterion function $\Sigma\Pi_i(z)$, the joint function which is to be maximized instantaneously (i.e. in planning time) by the choice of z^*. I propose as the Criterion Function actual profit, with a real-time adaptive search procedure to find t^*. Whether planned or realized profit is used as the Criterion Function, one difficulty is immediate: a free-entry competitive industry will in the long run generate zero profit for any level of z or t, including levels at which either polluters or pollutees may have closed down.

There are various ways of avoiding this difficulty, of which two are more or less equivalent.

(1) Fix the number of firms, as Groves (1976) does, and limit the analysis to the short run, so that at least one factor is fixed (as I think is implicit in Groves).

(2) Assume explicitly that the production functions exhibit everywhere decreasing marginal productivity to a

(single, homogeneous) variable input, as did Archibald and Wright (1976). It is then implicit that there exists a fixed factor and explicit that non-negative rents will be associated with positive outputs.[2] The number of firms may change (trivially) but the model does not encompass the long-run process of capital formation.

(3) In principle, one could build a free-entry genuinely long-run model, while retaining the assumption of some factor in inelastic supply (land, say, or coal seams) so that intra-marginal units earned rent.

For the purposes of this study, it is imperative that there be non-negative rents to monitor. I shall accordingly adopt the Archibald–Wright assumption. The analysis cannot extend to the Marshallian long run, but it proves that the number of firms can change in an interesting way. The reason for this may be briefly stated. I assume that the pollution, z, is – and is known to be – a "public bad" in the sense that the pollutee is affected by its total quantity, irrespective of source, and that its "consumption" by one pollutee accordingly affords no relief to the others. Each source must, however, be identified and strictly monitored in order that the tax may be levied on each polluter. I thus assume, with Baumol and Oates (1975), and Groves, that "there is a meter in every drain pipe," although I do not assume that the quantity of pollution is to be controlled directly by (for example) quotas or emission standards. (It is, of course, possible that the costs of monitoring, even without the cost of enforcing quantity controls, exceed the benefit from correction.[3] I can unfortunately see no way of knowing this *ex ante* and must disregard the matter.) What does not have to be known *ex ante* is the list of pollutees. Any firm may claim to be afflicted. We do not have to ask if the claim is fraudulent, or honest but exaggerated, or completely mistaken. The firm's profit may be added in without any question. If it is in fact invariant to z, its profit will simply be a constant, not affecting the maximum of $\Sigma \Pi_i$ at which t^* is determined. The only difficulty is the possibility of under-reporting: firms only slightly affected may not think it worth incurring the transactions costs of reporting.

An incentive to report might in fact be required; but I shall not pursue this matter.

We may notice here another piece of interesting information that is not required. Under the scheme to be proposed, not only does no one have to know any functions but the tax authority does not require even elementary knowledge of the technology (once, that is, it has determined that the case is suitable for application of the scheme proposed here, which is further discussed in section 4.6 below, and has identified the polluters). It is thus possible that an externality can be controlled (abated) with equal cost either "at source" or "on receipt." Archibald and Wright described such a technology as $(1,1)$, a technology in which abatement is nowhere possible as $(0,0)$, and one in which abatement is possible only at source as $(1,0)$. As will become apparent, the scheme proposed here has the property that the tax authority does not have to know which sort of technology, in the above sense, it is dealing with (although, in fact, it may costlessly find out as it monitors profits).

The four vital assumptions are (1) that firms do (somehow) maximize profits, (2) that the joint profit function satisfies appropriate concavity conditions, which are specified in section 4.6 below, (3) that profits (rents) are correctly reported, and (4) that there are no irreversibilities or indivisibilities in the abatement process.

4.3 The behavior of firms

The simplest rule of operation for a firm that wishes to maximize but has very limited information is that it adopts a simple feed-back algorithm, such as that suggested by Day (1967). We operate in discrete time, and assume that the firm knows the value of its choice variable, output, for the last two periods. It also knows the associated pay-off. If an action (change in choice variable) increases the pay-off, it repeats it; if not, it reverses. To ensure convergence, we need a "caution parameter" so that, in case of overshoot (a previously successful action has become unsuccessful), the reverse response is damped in magnitude. To get within a neighborhood of the maximum, we add a "satisficing parameter" such that, when the ratio of incremental pay-off to action falls below its value, the firm "freezes."

I assume that both polluters (henceforth called the steel industry) and pollutees (the flower industry) behave in the manner described by Day (1967). In particular, I assume that, in response to any tax rate on pollution, the steel industry can search in this manner for a point in the neighborhood of maximum profit. Similarly, I assume that, for any given pollution level, the flower industry can "feel its way."

Clearly if the behavior of firms is such that they get only within neighborhoods of maximum profit, the actual tax rate can be got only within a neighborhood of t^*. Thus our approximation to t^* is better the smaller are the firms' satisficing parameters: we cannot do better than the behavior of individual agents allows. Similarly, the scheme will work better the faster the firms converge and the less they oscillate. It would thus be helpful if they were better adapted: even if they continued to drive by the rear-vision mirror, they might learn better techniques of search, taking into account higher-order changes in pay-off and so on. They might even learn to use some "feed-forward" (see section 4.7 below). Even so, the simplest case serves the present illustrative purpose quite well.

At any given level of tax, the steel industry searches a fixed environment. While it is doing so, however, it is changing z (that is, the flower industry's environment). Thus if the flower industry's response rules and caution parameters are not well chosen, it is liable to oscillate in a tiresome manner. If, in fact, steel oscillates, then oscillations are forced upon flowers, but at least there is no feed-back to the steel industry. This matter will become clearer when the rules for the tax authority have been described and the scheme completed.

It is assumed that there is a "short" time period for the reporting of profits, and that this coincides with the firms' decision periods.

4.4 The control procedure

Given that the environment is stable, except for deliberate changes in the tax rate, and that profits are allowed to converge at each tax rate before it is changed again, we could in principle start to build up a picture of the joint profit function. (Procedures of this sort, usually to recover the cost functions, are used in some planning algorithms. See Arrow and Hurwicz, 1977, p. 13 *et seq.*, and references cited therein.) This would, however, entail a degree of sophistication quite out of keeping with the intentions of this chapter. Assuming always that the flow of pollution is being strictly monitored, and that taxes due are collected, we may institute a quite elementary procedure. We require a simple tax clerk provided with an adding machine and an algorithm for driving by the rear-vision mirror. It will save later repetition if I offer some detail of the procedure now.

We must start by endowing the tax clerk with a list of decision parameters.

(1)   He must know when reported profits (polluters' and pollutees') have converged "enough" to be regarded as maximal for any tax rate. We accordingly define a "convergence parameter" δ. Since absolute profits may be large money sums, it is convenient to make the convergence rule proportionate. Thus the clerk is to be instructed to regard profits as stationary whenever

$$\frac{\left(\sum_i \Pi_{i,h}(t) - \sum_i \Pi_{i,h-1}(t)\right)}{\sum_i \Pi_{i,h-1}(t)} \leqq \delta \qquad (4.1)$$

(where h is a decision-and-reporting period for the firms).

(2)   He must know by how much to change tax when a change is indicated. We give him an initial adjustment parameter, the (positive or negative) increment Δt.

(3)   In case of overshoot (profits fall in response to a change in tax in a direction previously successful) he must apply a "caution parameter" θ, $0 < \theta < 1$, to Δt as he "backs up."

(4)   He must be given a satisficing parameter ε to judge when t has converged closely "enough to" t^*. Again it is

convenient to put this into proportionate form. He is to be instructed to "stop" (freeze the tax rate) whenever

$$\left| \frac{\sum_i \Pi_i(t_\tau) + z_\tau t_\tau - \sum_i \Pi_i(t_{\tau-1}) - z_{\tau-1} t_{\tau-1}}{\sum_i \Pi_i(t_{\tau-1}) + z_{\tau-1} t_{\tau-1}} \right| \leqq \varepsilon. \quad (4.2)$$

Comparison of (4.1) and (4.2) will clarify the notation and the time periods involved. $\Pi_{i,h-1}(t), \Pi_{i,h}(t)$, and so on, form the sequence of profits earned by a firm, period by period, as it responds to a given tax rate t. $\Sigma_i \Pi_i(t_{\tau-1}) + z_{\tau-1} t_{\tau-1}, \Sigma_i \Pi_i(t_\tau) + z_\tau t_\tau$, and so on, form the sequence of maximal (within a neighborhood δ) profits earned by the firms in response to a sequence of tax rates plus the tax yield. In (4.2), the clerk's Criterion Function, tax yield has been added to profit. This is because, under normal accounting conventions, steel will deduct tax before reporting profit and, of course, the tax yield would appear as part of the joint profit if the firms were merged.

One should presumably assume that the system starts, in general, with $t=0$. Description of the tax clerk's rules is, however, much easier if one starts *in medias res*, without taking specific account of the first step. Starting from $t_0 = 0$ the first step may, of course, be very "jerky," and many periods be required for convergence of $\Pi_i(t_i)$ (and see the uncomfortable possibility discussed in section 4.6 below). Of course, the nearer the initial tax can be set to t^* the faster the whole system will converge: if someone can make an informed guess, adaptive behavior imposes less delay. In any case, we may present the rules which are to govern the behavior of the tax clerk.

1   Add up reported profit at the current tax rate t_τ each reporting period h, and consider 4.1 above. If the inequality is not satisfied, do nothing. If it is satisfied, go to 2.

2   Compare the value of the left-hand side of (4.1) with that recorded the "last time" profits converged (i.e. consider (4.2) above). If the inequality is satisfied (it has

converged to a satisficing neighborhood of t^* by (4.2)) go to 6. If the inequality is not satisfied, go to 3.

3   Is the algebraic value of the left-hand side of (4.2) positive or negative? If positive, go to 4, if negative go to 5.

4   You are going in the right direction. Repeat the adjustment and go to 1.

5   You have overshot and must back up. Change t by $\theta\Delta t$ of opposite sign to the last change, and go to 1. (Note: if you have overshot before, make the change $\theta^r\Delta t$ where r is the number of reversals.)

6   Maintain t at its current value, but continue to monitor profit each period. The inequality (4.1) may cease to be satisfied because of a change in the environment (tastes, technology, or relative prices). If this happens change t and go to 1. (Note: it is easier to guess in which direction to change t in this case if polluters' and pollutees' profits are summed separately, as we shall find in section 4.5 below that, for other reasons, they must be.)

We have the following delays in this system:

(a)   for the steel industry to converge, given any t, and present the flower industry with a stable environment,

(b)   for the flower industry to converge,

(c)   for the tax clerk to try again and wait out (a) and (b), before taking the next decision.

In the algorithm given above, (a) and (b) have been "run together" for simplicity of exposition. In fact, we should distinguish between convergence in steel and in flowers, and perhaps set separate convergence criteria, δ_1 and δ_2, say. (The interactions between steel, flowers, and the tax clerk are set out schematically in Figure 4.1 where output of steel is denoted by x, and that of flowers by y.)

For the firms' and the clerks' algorithms to converge, we assume, of course, that the profit functions are concave (which, if we relax our technological assumptions, they will not be: see section 4.6 below). Thus it is assumed that each firm's profit

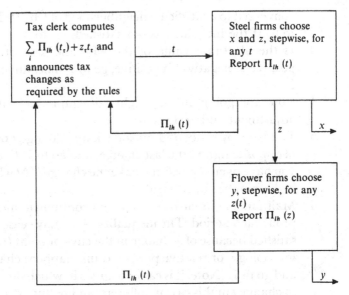

Figure 4.1   Chart of the algorithm

function is concave in its (non-negative) output for all $t > 0$. It is further assumed that z is monotonic decreasing in t, that profits in steel are monotonic decreasing in t, and that profits in flowers are monotonic decreasing in z and therefore increasing in t (up to that t, t' say, at which $z = 0$). Total profit, the sum of profits in steel and flowers, is of course assumed to have a global maximum at $t^* > 0$ (with $z^* \geq 0$) and, for convergence, total profit must be a pseudo-concave function of t.[4] For the interior maximum to exist, flower profits at $t^* > 0$ must, of course, exceed steel profits at $t = 0$ (it is assumed that profits in flowers are non-negative at $t = 0$; see below). Notice that, for $t \geq t' > t^*$, $z = 0$ and profits become invariant to t. Thus we can assume pseudo-concavity of total profit only over the domain $0 \leq t \leq t'$; and there does exist the possibility of an overshoot at the first step in the search process so large that z goes immediately to zero and the search stops at once at some $t > t'$. A "small" first step and adjustment Δt will guard against this possibility.

We note that the tax clerk does nothing (after announcing t) until flowers have converged. Similarly, after converging for t, steel has nothing to change until a new t is announced. There is no simultaneous feed-back from steel to clerk or from flowers to steel. This is analogous to the "relaxation" rules considered by Day and Tinney (1968) who show that the algorithm is convergent.[5]

4.5 Some difficulties with profit

Consideration of strategic behavior by agents subject to control by an iterative process is deferred to ch. 5. We must notice here, however, that the firms in both the steel and flower industries have an incentive to misreport profits. Steel producers may wish to show an exaggerated loss of profit as t increases, trying to send the signal "*we* are paying for the environment," and perhaps hoping to abate the process. Flower reporters may see a similar reason to under-report their gains. I have to assume that there exist well understood accounting conventions such that books can be audited, and "profit" be made an interpersonally consistent entity. We may threaten firms with audit, but need not always audit all firms. Consider a rule of the sort: "if the ith firm's reported change in profit from 'last time' is more than d standard deviations from the mean change in its industry, its books are to be audited and, if it is found to have been misreporting, its manager sent to Siberia." (It is now clear why profits in the two industries should be summed separately before they are fed into (4.2) above.) The firms have a "collective" incentive to misreport, but I submit that, under this rule, the non-cooperative solution to the prisoners' dilemma may be expected. Occasional random audit might help to keep the threat credible. It must, however, be admitted that this is one of the points, advertised in section 1.2 above, at which I appear to have abandoned the search for incentive compatibility and appealed for criminal sanctions. If the firms were publicly owned, and managers' rewards depended on profits, this problem might be resolved but, as we shall see, others would take its place.

It is necessary to recall that "profit," for present purposes, includes rent or quasi-rent to the (implicit) fixed factor: indeed, in a long-run competitive equilibrium all "profits" will be rents. Whether they appear as part of accounting profit or cost will depend on the accident of ownership. In the former case, there is no special problem. In the latter case, the tax clerk must be told how to identify that part of accounting cost which is to be added back when he sums the π_i.

In the long run, a free-entry CRS industry, which does not use a natural resource in limited supply will, of course, satisfy the zero-profit zero-rent condition at any level of control, whence this scheme cannot be applied. Sufficient assumptions to generate rents to monitor were discussed above. An obvious question is whether the scheme would work if only one of the two industries was able to earn rent. The answer is no. Suppose that steel could earn rent while a CRS free-entry flower industry always tended to zero profit. Then a pollution tax would always reduce rent in steel while the flower industry would show zero profit and rent in equilibrium: we should always receive the signal that the tax should be zero. If, on the other hand, the flower industry could earn rent while steel tended to zero profit, we should never stop short of the tax at which pollution was zero. Thus the very simple case used for illustrative purposes in this chapter depends on a particular industrial location pattern. If steel is a free-entry competitive industry, but rents are obtained by steel firms "here," perhaps because they have been able to impose costs on others with impunity here, we may wonder why they are not all here, or at least what conditions obtain in the rest of the supposedly "competitive" industry. Similarly, if the flower industry is competitive, we may wonder why any firms are "here" at all: presumably the costs of pollution are balanced against some other natural advantage (soil, perhaps). It seems, at least, that the simple upstream–downstream example may not be as simple as one might wish for the – simple – expository purposes of this chapter.

4.6 Technological difficulties

A chapter which is supposed to give a very simple example of an iterative control scheme, and display some of its properties, is not the place for a general discussion of the problem of non-convexities in the technology. Unfortunately, the subject cannot be entirely avoided here, if only because the assumption that the total profit function, $\Sigma\Pi_i$, is at least pseudo-concave is crucial.

It is well known now that externality problems can, in general, be regarded as examples of non-convexity problems (see Starrett, 1972, and, for a particularly lucid exposition, Heller and Starrett, 1975). This is not the immediate issue. Problems of non-convexity have so far been ruled out by assumption. Unfortunately, these assumptions may well break down and, with them, the corrective scheme proposed here. We may easily see how this may happen.

Consider Figure 4.2, where inputs to the flower industry of the variable resource R_y are measured on the horizontal axis and the flower output y on the vertical. The production function assumed in section 4.2 above is illustrated by $g(R_y,z_0)$, $g(R_y,z_1)$ and $g(R_y,z_2)$. (It is, of course, assumed that the production function for steel, $x=f(R_x)$, is of the same general form.) With pollution at z_2, say, and the price of flowers in terms of units of R given by the slope of PQ, the flower industry produces OS and earns rent OP. It is unfortunately perfectly possible that at a yet higher level of pollution, z_3 say, the production function for flowers takes the form of $g(R_y,z_3)$: OB resources have to be used up "first" in fighting pollution before any flowers can be grown at all. At a price lower than that given by the slope of OT, no flowers are produced, since rents will be negative. (As drawn in Figure 4.2, the price of flowers on OT is slightly higher than on PQ, but this is immaterial.) We have a discontinuity in price–quantity space at pollution level z_3, and a non-convexity in output–z-space of the sort illustrated by Heller and Starrett (1975). Notice that matters are no better if $g(R_y,z_3)$ has the form indicated by one of the broken lines in Figure 4.2. The consequence of such a non-convexity in the technology is, of course, to violate our assumptions of concavity of each firm's profit function in its own (non-negative) output and of pseudo-concavity of total profit in the tax rate.

For the corrective scheme proposed here this (technologically

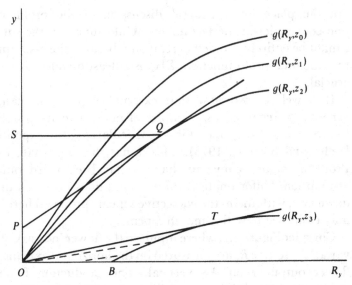

Figure 4.2   The technology of an externality problem

reasonable) possibility poses a serious difficulty. Suppose that, before any corrective measures are taken, the levels of pollution and relative prices are such that no flowers are produced, whereas at the optimal level of pollution flowers would be produced. Unless there is some past history ("we used to grow lovely flowers here before those stinkers came along") it may not even be realized that correction is called for. Suppose, however, that it is. An initial level of t that is "too small" may simply reduce profit in the steel industry without inducing production of flowers at all (reaching, that is, as far as point T in Figure 4.2). The response to the first step in the iteration would thus signal retreat from the direction of the global maximum.

It follows that the control discussed here depends upon one of two conditions being satisfied. The first, assumed up to now, is that initially the system is not in the non-convex no-flowers region. The second is that it is, but that this is recognized, and that the first trial tax rate is set high enough to jump over the discontinuity. This in turn requires more information, intelligence – and daring – than "we" should probably attribute to ourselves. It is plainly possible that, as a consequence of non-convexity, there are whole unknown and unexplored areas of the technology.

We recall now the assumption made in section 4.2 above, that there are no indivisibilities (non-convexities) and irreversibilities in the abatement technology. If there are, or perhaps just large adjustment costs, experimenting with non-optimal tax rates in real time may impose serious costs. We may conjecture that the larger are such non-convexities, the larger are individual firms likely to be, whence the more "likely" (in some loose sense) are they to be able to recover the information they need for internal planning, instead of merely driving by the rear-vision mirror. If firms have this information (or reasonable opportunity to get it) then the proposals of Groves (1976) and Groves and Loeb (1975) (incentive for disclosure of the information; solution in planning time) seem more appropriate than the trial-and-error method we have discussed. If we are faced with indivisibilities and ignorance (or, at least, very costly information) it is not obvious what control may be appropriate.

4.7 Faster control processes

It must by now be apparent that this "simplest" example is highly artificial. Nonetheless, we may ask how the process might be speeded up.

Consider first the behavior of private agents (firms, here). I have emphasized above that the speed to convergence of the whole process is bounded by firms' speed of convergence to local maxima. They may well do better than has so far been assumed. There is a natural selection argument for thinking that they must at least do "well enough" (Nelson and Winter, 1982). With some memory and feed-forward, not to mention improved hill-climbing algorithms, they may do much better. It should not take steel firms long to realize, if they do not already know it, that their profit-maximizing (satisficing) output levels are negatively correlated with the pollution tax (and abatement levels, if any, positively correlated). This is memory. Then feed-forward speeds up their response: when the tax is changed they can start a search process in the right direction without waiting for feed-*back*. We may well suppose that they can learn to cope in the same way with other important features of their environment (forecasts of GNP, say). The possibilities of memory and feed-forward for flowers are particularly attractive. If flower firms grasp the fact that *their* profits depend on the tax rate, then feed-forward can give their behavior quite a sophisticated appearance although it is still purely adaptive (cf. Rosen, 1975).

Consider next the tax clerk's behavior. He clearly can be programmed to use more efficient hill-climbing techniques although, as we shall see in ch. 5, only at increasing risk of leaving the control open to strategic behavior. (Better techniques are discussed in, for example, Marglin, 1969 and Arrow and Hurwicz, 1977; they are intended for planning time, but can clearly be adapted to "clerk's time.") We may even be able to employ some feed-forward in setting the tax. Experience should tell us at least some of the comparative static properties of the system, which may well not be qualitatively determined. Thus experience may reveal, what cannot be known *a priori*, which way the tax should be changed if, say, the abatement technology is improved. The tax clerk can then be directed to start a new search in the right direction (feed-forward) without any alteration in his simple wiring. Evidently, potentially useful and cheap information is lost if the tax clerk is not directed to sum (and report) flower profits and steel profits separately.

4.8   Relation of the example to Second Best

In spite of the artificiality of the upstream–downstream problem, it is worth considering the appropriateness of the control system discussed here if the best that the whole economy can attain is a Second Best. What setting the "optimal" tax does here is impose the efficiency price (tax) on the otherwise unpriced intermediate input. The "classical" (Lipsey and Lancaster, 1957) setting of the Second-Best problem is in a world with a strictly convex technology and convex preferences displayed by a "representative" consumer. It is fairly obvious, and easy to show,[6] that, in this case, if, and only if, the distortion is strictly confined to a final (consumer) good, competitive, or efficiency, pricing in factor markets is still optimal. This might encourage us to think that, even if there is a distortion in product pricing elsewhere in the economy, our optimal tax is still Second Best optimal. This is not really true. The tax can be set only for given conditions in the two industries concerned. These conditions do not, of course, imply given outputs, but certainly imply given input supplies *and* output demands. If any of these are "wrong," as they will be if there is an uncorrected distortion elsewhere in the economy, the efficiency tax on the intermediate product (the pollution) will be correspondingly "wrong." This makes no difference whatever to the tax-setting process: but if, and only if, prices in the rest of the economy are properly adjusted, will it lead to the "right" tax rate. The same argument applies, *mutatis mutandis*, if there is an uncorrected (monopoly) distortion in flowers or steel. The tax-setting process yields, if other assumptions are satisfied, the efficiency price, but neither First nor Second Best. Whether any purpose is achieved by using processes piecemeal in an economy with uncorrected distortions elsewhere is quite another matter.

4.9   Properties of the control process reviewed

It remains to compare the properties of the control discussed here with the list given in section 3.3 above:

1A   Supplied by the Criterion Function $\Sigma\Pi_i$.
2A.1   See algorithm.
2A.2   Criterion Function.
3A   This list itself.
3A.1   Depends critically upon our assumptions about the technology (see section 4.6 above).
3A.2   See algorithm.
3A.3   Monotonicity is *not* assured: see algorithm.
4A.1   Incentive compatability is assured by one-period (myopic) profit maximization.
4A.2   The matter of false reporting of profit was discussed in

section 4.4 above. Consideration of strategic behavior is otherwise deferred to ch. 5.

4A.3   See algorithm.

4A.4   See section 4.5 above.

We might, I suppose, say "so far, so good," *but* the application of this chapter is very limited, indeed stylized, *and* two problems demand attention: the possibilities for strategic behavior, and of non-convexities in the technology. The former is considered in ch. 5; the latter is deferred to Part III.

5

Second application of the control process: Lerner's Problem

5.1 Planning, regulation, and agency

I call this "Lerner's Problem" although it has emerged in recent literature under other labels, particularly "The Incentive Problem for a Soviet-style Manager." I think that a brief digression to explain my title may be in order.

I imagine that many students of my generation were brought up, as I was, to speak (in an oral tradition) of "Lerner–Lange socialism." Even a casual re-reading of their work (Lerner, 1944; Lange, 1936/7) is sufficient to show that the hyphen is inappropriate. Lange's contribution was to suggest that the Central Planning Board (henceforth CPB) should announce prices rather than quantities. This is in the tradition of Taylor (1929) rather than of Barone (1908). The advantages of announcing prices rather than quantities were two, one perhaps trivial, the other more serious. The first is that it might be technically easier to solve the dual than the primal problem. This, we now know, is a little trivial: if we have the information and computational facilities to solve one, we can solve the other. The second advantage is important. Lange, like Taylor, thought that by announcing only prices, the CPB could achieve a large measure of decentralization: *given* prices, economic agents could be left to "get on with it," maximizing on their own account, and thus reproducing, or "choosing," the quantities which would have emerged from a solution to the primal problem, without any need for concern with implementation.

Lerner took decentralization much further. In his model, the

CPB is redundant: neither the primal nor the dual planning problems need explicit solution. He depended on contemporary welfare economics, and took marginal cost pricing as the objective, or "Rule." Thus no interference was necessary in industries in which perfect competition is viable. Elsewhere, what was required was nationalization of firms, and the appointment of managers who would obey the Rule: thus very thorough decentralization, the antithesis of the "Command Economy."

This raises two, not one, obvious problems. The first is that "elsewhere" (perfect competition not viable) is, we may think, just in those activities in which the technology is non-convex. Lerner was well aware of this. He relied on what we might call the "strong interpretation" of what subsequently (Arrow, 1951a) became called the Second Theorem of Welfare Economics, namely that even in the case of non-convexities considerations of efficiency and of distribution can be divorced. Unfortunately, the "strong interpretation" (which is *not* Arrow's) is wrong. I discuss this in Part III. Here I wish to address the other problem that Lerner left unsolved.

This problem is obvious: what incentive has a manager to obey the Rule? Indeed, how should we know if he did not, and what should we do about it? To know, we should have to know as much, or almost as much, about the enterprise as the manager did, and to enforce the Rule we should require some police powers (see section 1.2 above). This would imply that the promised decentralization was in fact a sham. Lerner was not unaware of this problem, but he did not address it. It has, as I have already noted, been addressed in more recent literature under the label of "Incentives for the Soviet Manager." I shall explore this solution in this chapter. First, however, there is yet another obvious problem.

Let us interpret "we" as above. We are clearly the principals, with an objective, and some powers, whether of property or prescription, to enter a contract. The manager (whether of an "enterprise," firm, or plant: I shall not distinguish here) is equally clearly an agent. So, we may ask, why is the management-incentive problem not regarded as a principal–agent problem, and treated under that label? It clearly is, in spirit, a principal–agent problem, but the formal structure is different.

In the formal principal–agent problem, it is assumed that we, the principals, have an objective function, a maximand. It is further assumed that the constraint is offered by the agent's unobservable, unpoliceable, but rationally self-interested behavior. The constraint can thus conveniently be formulated in terms of a first-order condition for his utility maximization. (Since I shall not be concerned now with the formal principal–agent problem, it is not necessary to consider the technical difficulties associated with this approach.) What I shall continue to call Lerner's Problem has a quite different structure. In place of a maximand, we have a Rule (marginal cost pricing) derived from a prior maximization problem (welfare). The managerial-incentive problem can be forced into the formal structure of a conventional principal–agent problem, but the structure has to be imposed. Thus a maximand must be found. This can be done by assuming (for example) that we wish the manager to maximize output given some previously determined resource constraint. Neary (1987) shows how this may be done – and, by implication, perhaps the limits of this approach. In the work on implementation of the Rule it is, however, also assumed that the agent, or manager, has only one argument in his utility function, his income or reward. This assumption is made for "simplicity," and apparently thought to be relatively innocuous but, as we shall see, it is critical. On these assumptions, iterative procedures for setting the manager's reward function have been proposed. Let us now consider them.

The recent literature on iterative procedures for setting the parameters of the manager's reward function starts with Domar (1974). Unfortunately, we now encounter what I can only call an anomaly in the literature, perhaps more than one. Setting the reward structure for a Soviet manager, or a Lerner manager, *or* controlling "regulated industries" (which, in some countries, will be exclusively public utilities, and perhaps some means of transport) are at least closely related matters, as are the principal–agent problem and, very generally, problems of control, or even contracting, with limited, indeed asymmetric,

information. Yet these subjects seem not to have been considered together, as is made very clear in the survey by Besanko and
Sappington (1987), *Designing Regulatory Policy with Limited
Information*. Works following Domar, particularly by Tam,
Finnsinger and Vogelsang, and Gravelle are cited and discussed
(for complete references, see Besanko and Sappington, 1987 and
below) but Domar's contribution is not mentioned. For that
matter, neither is Lerner's or, more generally, the "economics of
socialism."

It seems that there is some difficulty over problem classifica-
tion, or filing, on which I propose to spend little time. We may, if
we wish, call our whole class of problems problems of limited
information, which indeed they are, or problems of agency,
which indeed they also are. Whether we call some subset of them
problems of regulation or of control is immaterial. It is, however,
worth noting that it is traditional and usual in the regulation
literature to use the aggregate consumers' surplus criterion (or
some convex combination of consumers' and producers' surplus), which I do not. Such a criterion is less commonly used in
the literature on managerial incentives – in which, indeed, we
frequently find appeal to Lerner's Rule. I shall not offer a
detailed history of the discussion following Domar, whence, for
consistency and autonomy, I shall adopt my own notation. In
particular, a superscript bar on a variable (e.g. $\bar{x}$) will denote an
optimal value of the variable for the agent setting it, whereas a
superscript star (e.g. x^*) will denote a value which we think is
(socially) optimal. The object of the exercise is, of course, to
make "stars and bars" coincide – that is, to enlist self-interest in
pursuit of what is thought to be socially optimal, and obviate the
need for policemen (see section 1.2 above).

Domar's cue was apparently not Lerner's work but a
suggestion in a speech of Khrushchev that, instead of being set
targets (quantity planning) Soviet managers be offered reward
functions. Khrushchev indeed proposed that the rewards include a bonus on output *and* on profit (a revolutionary notion!).
Domar took up the question of how to set the parameters of such
a reward function by a step-wise procedure.

If we follow Lerner, managers have to be instructed, or specially rewarded, only in activities in which perfect competition is not viable. Thus we have to deal exclusively with enterprises facing downward sloping demand curves for their products. This in turn suggests size, increasing returns: in other words, non-convexity of the technology (as Lerner did know). In the algebra that follows, it will be apparent that nothing depends on the second derivative of the cost function – although, to postpone yet further the non-convexity problem while taking the opportunity to consider strategic behavior, it may be assumed that marginal cost is either constant or increasing. It is necessary to assume that the demand curve is downward sloping (and obvious that I assume both functions to be twice differentiable). Each firm produces only a single product.

Let the manager's reward function be

$$R = a + bq + c\Pi \tag{5.1}$$

where a, b, and c are parameters to be determined, q is output (sales) and Π is profit. Profit is given by

$$\Pi = qf(q) - g(q) \tag{5.2}$$

where $f(q)$ is the (inverse) demand function and $g(q)$ is the cost function. The manager's decision variable is q. Comparison of (5.1) and (5.2) makes it clear that manager's reward should be included in the cost function itself: it will indeed appear in the derivatives. To include it would greatly complicate the algebra. I ignore it to avoid complication, and in the hope that the error is not quantitatively important. In any case there are, as we shall see below, more fundamental problems with this approach. To maximize reward, the manager will wish to set $\bar{q}$ such that

$$\frac{dR}{dq} = b + c\{qf'(q) + f(q) - g'(q)\} = 0. \tag{5.3}$$

Evidently, the constant a in the reward function has dropped out (like fixed cost) and may be considered later. We want q^* such that price equals marginal cost, or $f(q) = g'(q)$. Substituting this into (5.3) gives the condition for equalizing barred and

starred values. (We may reasonably call this "Domar's trick.")
This is that the parameters be set such that

$$\frac{b}{c} = -qf'(q) \tag{5.4}$$

which is necessarily positive. (Evidently the term (b/c) could be
starred here; but let us avoid clutter.)

How can b/c be chosen to satisfy (5.4)? We must either have an
unlikely amount of information, or adopt some step-wise
procedure, as Domar suggested.[1]

5.2   Iterative control

Let us next construct an iterative control process to set b/c to
satisfy (5.4). Some elements of the control may seem for the
moment arbitrary, but will be explained below. It is not, I am
sure, necessary to set out the algorithm in all the detail provided
in ch. 4.

We have a slight initial difficulty. (b/c) is only a ratio, but
numerical values for the individual parameters are required.
One of the two parameters must be predetermined somehow.
Consider the case of constant marginal cost. At q^* we shall have
$\Pi = 0$, whence the manager's reward will be $a + bq$. We may
therefore set b at some "guessed" value for appropriate managerial compensation (the parameter a may be adjusted after-
wards if our guess is bad: see section 5.4 below). So we start the
process at fixed b_0 and a trial value of c, say c_0. For expositional
simplicity, let us suppose that we start at $q < q^*$ which may or
may not be the private profit-maximizing q. It does not at all
matter to the control system on which side we do start, but it is
clearly convenient that we know. It may seem paradoxical that
we could use a bonus on profit, c, to "lure" a manager to a point
at which there is no profit but, as we shall see, if we can make the
control strategy-proof, that is exactly what we shall do.

Now the manager is given time to adjust to b_0 and c_0, precisely
as before, and the corresponding values p_0 and q_0 are recorded.
(We could clearly record profit and cost as well, and might wish
to.) Here we make an essential assumption, similar to that about

the honest reporting of profit required above: p_0 and q_0 *must* be market-clearing values, readings from the demand curve. I know of no way of guaranteeing this, and unhappily suppose that it might be necessary to police order books and inventories. At the beginning of the next period the clerk announces a new value of c, c_1. Let us suppose, arbitrarily for the moment, that the clerk is instructed to set $c_1 = c_0 - \Delta c$, where Δc is the shift value predetermined by us. The clerk now records the pair p_1 and q_1, and can compute Δp and Δc for (approximate) comparison with (5.4). This process simply continues until (5.4) is satisfied, or at least within the limit of some satisficing parameter. In the case of overshoot, the back up is again $\theta^\rho \Delta c$, where $0 < \theta < 1$, θ is predetermined by us, and ρ is the number of reversals. If marginal cost is constant, then $\Pi = 0$ at q^*. If it is increasing, $\Pi > 0$, the manager collects the bonus $c_t \Pi(q^*)$, and we collect the "rent tax" $(1 - c_t) \Pi(q^*)$ (where, of course, $c_t = c_0 - t\Delta c$ where t is the number of steps before convergence, with appropriate adjustment in the case of overshoot).

5.3 Uniqueness and convergence

This outline of the control process obviously leaves many matters unresolved, among them uniqueness, and the possibility of strategic behavior.

Convergence seems obvious, but monotonicity has explicitly not been guaranteed. We shall see why when we consider strategic behavior in section 5.5 below. First let us check both that the control at least "goes in the right direction," and that the (approximate) solution is unique (a matter that seems to have been rather neglected in the literature cited above).

For the former, first notice that

$$\frac{d^2R}{dq^2} = \frac{d^2\Pi}{dq^2} = qf''(q) + 2f'(q) - g''(q) < 0 \tag{5.5}$$

is the usual second-order condition. Now, starting from the left, we want $\bar{q}$ to increase as c falls – to be, that is, a decreasing function of c. Totally differentiating (5.3) with respect to c and q, we have

$$\frac{\partial \bar{q}}{\partial c} = -\frac{MR - MC}{c d^2 \Pi / dq^2} \tag{5.6}$$

(using (5.3) and (5.5)). If (5.3) is satisfied and $b > 0$, $MR - MC$ must be negative. The denominator must be negative by (5.5), whence the whole expression is negative as required.

Thus the myopic maximizing manager is indeed led in the right direction. It remains to check that the stopping rule in (5.4) gives a unique solution: we do not want a control that may accidentally stick at the wrong place.

A diagram (Figure 5.1) may help. We wish to show both sides of (5.4) here as functions of real, or "iteration," time, which is measured on the horizontal axis. Now, b is a dollar quantity, so much per unit, and c is a fraction, whence b/c is measured in dollars. So too is $-qf'(q)$. So, with \$ on the vertical axis, both may be displayed in this space. For diagrammatic convenience, I have drawn both as continuous functions of time, t, although t is discrete and both are really step functions. This matters only in the overshoot region, with which we are not now concerned. With b_0 fixed, and c_t decreasing in t, b/c is a positive function of t, increasing without limit. $-qf'(q)$ is also positive. We have already seen that q is decreasing in c, whence increasing in t, so we may expect $-qf'(q)$ to be increasing in t but, without imposing more restrictions on the demand curve (on $f''(q)$, that is), we cannot rule out the possibility that it "wriggles." What we do know is that it cannot increase without limit. So long as the budget constraint binds on consumers, there is a finite limit on q (at which $f(q) = 0$). So $-qf'(q)$ must have "something" of the general slope shown in Figure 5.1.

As shown, the two functions have a unique intersection. This is clearly not necessary. That $-qf'(q)$ "wriggles" enough to cross and recross b/c may seem "unlikely," but it is clearly quite possible that there be two intersections or none ($-qf'(q)$ lying everywhere below b/c). It is, of course, perfectly possibly that a marginal cost curve lies everywhere above an arbitrarily chosen demand curve, or intersects it twice (in the U-shaped case). The simplest possible example – constant marginal cost and linear demand – does, of course, give a unique intersection. In the case

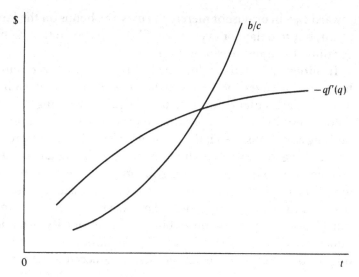

Figure 5.1   Parameters and targets

of a U-shaped cost curve and a double intersection, we may assume that the system starts at a higher q than that which minimizes profits (where, indeed, sufficient conditions for managerial maximization would not be satisfied). If there exists no intersection, presumably the activity was not viable in the first place.

5.4   Monotonicity and strategy-proofness

To set Δc as an arbitrary shift constant, as was done above, may seem crude. Clearly the larger it is, the greater is the possibility of overshoot, whereas the smaller it is, the slower is the process. There is a trade-off here. Furthermore, it is natural to ask if the process could be speeded up, even smoothed, by making Δc at least in part endogenous, making it respond to Δq, or even $\Delta^2 q$. It could, of course, but only at the risk of inviting strategic behavior by the manager, as we shall see.

Consider a step in the process, with given parameter values, and a response $\bar{q}$. Intuition strongly suggests that there may be parameter values, and a value of the discount rate, such that it would pay the manager to set $q < \bar{q}$, sacrificing some part of the reward $b_0\bar{q}$, in order not merely to enjoy the bonus on the larger profit, but to delay, or even "freeze" the process so that he may continue to enjoy his share of profit.

Intuition might be right, but the control process discussed here in fact leaves the manager helpless. Δc is predetermined, and the clerk's algorithm tells him to go on reducing c by this amount until (5.4) is (approximately) satisfied. He responds to nothing else. Thus even if the manager tries to freeze the process, not altering quantity at all, he will be "hit" again by a Δc change. We make the system strategy-proof by putting parameter changes out of the manager's control; we invite strategic behavior by endogenizing them. To make the system work more quickly, or increase the probability of monotonicity, we might "doctor" Δc in other ways. Thus after an initial "large" Δc_1, we might (for example) instruct the clerk to proceed as $\Delta c_t = \alpha^t \Delta c_1$, $0 < \alpha < 1$.

The literature already cited offers examples in which parameter values, or their changes, are indeed endogenous. That our intuition is then right is proved in one case by Finnsinger and Vogelsang (1985), and in another by Gravelle (1985). It does not seem necessary to rehearse these proofs. The matter may be more simply illustrated by considering one suggestion (Tam, 1981).[2] Here the reward is given at each step by

$$R_t = \alpha_t \Pi_t + \beta_t(-p) \tag{5.7}$$

with the adjustment rule

$$\beta_t/\alpha_t = q_{t-1}. \tag{5.8}$$

The intention is to set a "negative bonus" on price, which is to depend on the previous period's output. This system is clearly open to strategic behavior, as has been shown. We may show that it is not viable in a rather simpler way. Suppose that a manager is fully aware of the rules written in (5.7) and (5.8), and decides to look for the $\bar{q}$ which will give a global maximum of R. We may easily see that such a $\bar{q}$ does not exist. Suppose that it did. Then we should have, at a global-maximizing equilibrium, $\bar{q} = q_t = q_{t-1} \ldots$. Substituting into (5.8), we have $\beta = \alpha q$ (suppressing time subscripts). A global maximum would thus be

$$\max_{q} R = \alpha\Pi - \alpha q f(q). \tag{5.9}$$

Differentiating, we find that this requires

$$qf'(q) + f(q) - g'(q) - qf'(q) - f(q) = 0 \tag{5.10}$$

or

$$-g'(q) = 0.$$

I see no point in speculating on how such a system might actually behave when manipulated by a well-informed and intelligent manager. Nor do I see any point in concerning ourselves further with other schemes that use endogenous variables, or some transforms of them, to regulate adjustments in the control process.

We must, I think, conclude that there is indeed a trade-off, between a crude process that does not ensure monotonicity, but is strategy-proof, and one that is better behaved only if the manager is myopic.

Let us now remember that we have neglected the parameter a, the constant in the reward function. In view of the above, we may conclude that we may set a any way we please so long as it is not a function of q! "Any way" clearly includes setting it to ensure that the manager does at least get his opportunity cost – correcting, that is, for a "bad guess" about the value of the reward $b_0 q^*$ (or even $c_i \Pi(q^*)$). Thus the constant might, in fact, turn out to be negative.

I have not formally considered the "overhead cost" case, which has taken up so much of the literature, that in which $g''(q) < 0$ and $\Pi(q^*) < 0$. None of the foregoing algebra would need alteration, but the story would be seriously incomplete without consideration of how the loss is to be made up, by a standing charge or otherwise. I shall continue to defer these general problems of non-convexity to ch. 9.

5.5 Uncertainty

It is now high time to introduce uncertainty into the model: after all, it is not easy otherwise to offer any formal means of justifying the satisficing parameter introduced above. With uncertainty formally introduced, it should be possible to suggest a rule for setting this parameter, providing sufficient tolerance to save the control from hunting, but ensuring that the process is restarted if any serious shift occurs. Unfortunately, the consequences of introducing uncertainty are too serious to make this piece of "fine-tuning" worth pursuing.

I contrasted in section 5.1 above the structure of the control problem addressed here with that of the principal–agent problem, and noted that in the present case the manager's utility function is assumed to have his pecuniary reward as its sole argument. We may introduce uncertainty without altering that assumption, but it is an uninteresting exercise unless we allow him to be risk-averse. If he is risk-neutral his behavior is unchanged: if he is risk-averse, not only is his behavior changed but the Rule itself requires amendment.

It is amazingly easy to show this. It is necessary only to follow Sandmo (1971), making the small amendments required by the reward function and the downward sloping demand curve. I shall follow him in placing the disturbance term on the demand function only. The cost function might well suffer disturbance instead, or as well. Empirically, this is probably a reasonable assumption: machine breakdown, absenteeism, materials supply, and so on. Nonetheless, the assumption that only demand suffers disturbance is much more tractable, and quite enough to establish our results. I shall further simplify by assuming that the disturbance is normally distributed about a zero mean. It is convenient to write

$$p = \phi(q) + \varepsilon \tag{5.11}$$

with

$$E[p] = \phi(q)$$

in place of Sandmo's $E[p] = \mu$. Thus, maintaining the reward structure assumed above, the manager is assumed to wish to find q such that, at any parameter values, it maximizes

$$E[U(R)] = E[U\{a + bq + c(q\phi(q) + \varepsilon q - g(q))\}]. \tag{5.12}$$

Setting the first derivative equal to zero, and re-arranging, we have the precise analogue of Sandmo's result:

$$E[U'(R)\{c\varepsilon\}] = E[U'(R')\{cg'(q) - b - c(q\phi'(q) + \phi(q))\}].$$
(5.13)

Again, following Sandmo, and using the fact that risk-aversion implies $E[U] \le U[E]$, we have

$$c(g'(q) - \phi(q)) \ne 0$$

or $MC < p$. This will be true for the $\bar{q}$ chosen for any parameters. It will accordingly be true when the process has been stopped by (5.4).

Before considering the implications of this result, we may conveniently reproduce another Sandmo result. He found that, on the assumption of diminishing risk-aversion, the firm's short-run equilibrium output is not invariant to fixed cost: it can be increased by a subsidy and reduced by a lump-sum tax. Here the constant a in the manager's reward function is the analogue of fixed cost in the profit function; and, by an argument exactly analogous to Sandmo's, it can be shown that, assuming declining absolute risk-aversion, we have $\partial \bar{q}/\partial a > 0$. The intuition of this is, I think, clear: the better-off manager is less risk-averse, and, accordingly, does not demand so high a "cushion" between his $\bar{q}$ and the value which would maximize the expectation of the reward.

Now, what has happened? We have changed the environment (no certainty); we have changed the manager's objective (he is assumed to be risk-averse); we have changed neither the control nor the target (the Rule: First-Best pricing). There is evidently a "mismatch." The obvious candidates are the control and the Rule (both unchanged). Consider the control first. It might perhaps be re-designed to accommodate risk-averse behavior (I have not tried) *but* we should require information quite in excess of what has so far been assumed, and quite contrary to our decentralizing intent. At the very least, we should require some revelation mechanism to discover a measure of the concavity of the utility function of any manager (or candidate for the position). I do not think this worth pursuing, particularly because it is the Rule itself that is inappropriate here.

If this manager's environment is risky, it is only reasonable to suppose that the environment is risky for all agents in the economy. In this case, as is well known (thanks mainly, I believe, to the work of Arrow), First Best is not generally attainable. Even if the set of markets were complete, incomplete information, of which the "moral hazard" problem is the best known example, precludes optimal risk-sharing, whence the best attainable is a Second Best. The Rule (marginal-cost pricing) is, as we know, nothing but a first-order condition from a prior maximization problem, maximization of welfare in a certain environment. There is thus no good reason why we should wish to enforce it in those sectors in which the installation of Lerner's managers, or any other managerial or pricing device, might allow us to. "Piecemeal" welfare economics is further considered below. First, however, let us extend the manager's utility function a little.

5.6   Effort-aversion

If the manager is assumed to be risk-averse, there is no obvious reason why he should not also be assumed to be "effort-averse." (We could, if it would serve any purpose, measure effort-aversion just as risk-aversion is measured.) Introducing effort – or leisure – as an argument of the manager's utility function yields, of course, the function usually attributed to the risk-averse agent in specification of the principal–agent problem. We still, however, have no maximand, only the Rule.

The manager's utility function may now be written as $U(R,e)$, where e denotes effort, and, of course, we assume $U_R > 0, U_e < 0$. What matters is the assumption that naturally accompanies this, that output depends, in part at least, on the manager's effort. This, in the present context, is most easily specified in terms of the cost function, so assume that $C = C(q,e)$, $C_q > 0, C_e < 0$. Clearly the manager's pecuniary reward is now in part dependent on his own effort, so we may write $R = R(e,\cdot)$, $R_e > 0$. It is now trivial to derive, as a first-order condition for his utility maximization, the usual: $U_R/U_e = -1/R_e$.

Let us not waste time trying to amend the control: the difficulties are more fundamental. First of all, if $C = C(q,e)$ cost minimization is not well defined. It is, at best, some lower boundary to a family of cost curves (for different levels of e), to be approached, perhaps, at some physical and psychological limits to e. This is not very satisfactory. Worse, if cost minimization is not well defined, neither can be marginal cost. It is, of course, given by C_q, but evaluated at what value of e? We could, I suppose, make some strong separability assumption, but with what empirical justification I do not know. If marginal cost is not well defined, then the Rule is operationally empty.

If, further, it is assumed that everyone, not only the manager, is effort-averse (enjoys leisure) then the Rule is irrelevant: it is a first-order condition of an over-simplified maximization problem, the standard problem of maximizing welfare subject to the technology and endowment constraints ("full employment"). The more general maximization problem, allowing that agents may differ in their tastes, and may be heterogeneous as inputs, requires, as is well known, the condition $U_R^i/U_e^i = -1/R_e^i$ for all agents i. It is not obvious that this can be expressed in, or achieved by, any simple Rule. It is sometimes alleged that the condition will be satisfied in perfect competition; but this cannot be supposed to hold without any specification of the information and incentive structure within the firm. The result is that our discussion of methods of implementation of simple welfare rules has revealed only their severe limitations.

There is perhaps one last addendum worth making. "Marginal cost" is, of course, a convenient partial-equilibrium notion: pending solution of the general equilibrium problem, we do not know factor prices. This difficulty can be handled in a quite straightforward manner. Thus Brown and Heal (1979) and (1980), in their work on marginal cost pricing in non-convex economies, are careful to define "marginal cost" in terms of the slope of the production possibility frontier. This does not remedy the problems connected with risk, risk-aversion, and effort-aversion.

6

Third example of the control process: implementation of a second-best solution[1]

6.1 A Second-Best problem

The object of ch. 6 is not, I fear, to offer any serious solution to the general problem of the Second Best. It has three much less ambitious objects. The first is to suggest a new use for a familiar Criterion Function, the simple "cost–benefit" criterion of the project-evaluation literature (see Hammond, 1980). The second is to clear up operationally the old question of which definition of complementarity is appropriate in dealing with Second-Best solutions (on which see Corlett and Hague, 1954; Meade, 1955a and 1955b; and of course Lipsey and Lancaster, 1957). The third is to illustrate the use of adaptive control methods in a general rather than, as hitherto, a purely partial-equilibrium model.

We have had occasion to notice, in ch. 5, two familiar reasons for thinking that the standard First-Best solution is unattainable and/or undesirable: aversion to risk and preference for leisure. In the explicit Second-Best literature neither of these difficulties has been addressed: it has rather been assumed that the reason for First Best being unattainable is lack of instruments: that the government will not alter a tax or tariff, or cannot control an important monopolist. Here I shall follow the Second-Best literature: for illustrative purposes, I shall ignore both risk and effort. First Best will be unattainable due only to lack of instruments with which to control a monopolist; and, though a certain non-convexity in the technology will be assumed, it will be only to facilitate exposition. There is a further compelling reason for regarding the model of this chapter as for "display purposes only."

In the standard welfare literature, both that from which First-Best Rules are derived, and that which demonstrates the problem of Second Best, the convenient fiction – or aggregate – of a "Representative Consumer" is adopted. It has recently been made clear that the aggregation conditions required are so restrictive that the Representative Consumer can no longer be regarded as more than a device for expositional purposes.[2] I shall assume a representative consumer in this chapter, for the sole purpose of displaying the three objects listed above. It will, of course, be noticed that the cost-benefit criterion used here relies on the representative consumer as much as it does in the standard work on project evaluation.

Two distinct problems have been identified in the literature on Second Best. The first is to identify what *direction* of change in the control instruments will lead to a Pareto-improvement. The second is to estimate the *magnitude* of the change required to reach the Second-Best optimum itself. The answer to the second question has usually been that we cannot know, and must therefore content ourselves with a small change (improvement) for fear of overshoot. It does, therefore, seem worthwhile to show that an iterative approach, entirely in terms of easily observable quantities, can lead to the required magnitudes of the control variables. As for direction, that will turn out to depend on a suitable and operational definition of substitutability and complementarity.

I offer the simplest Second Best problem that Davidson and I were able to devise. The uncontrollable monopolist is the proprietor of Cournot's mineral spring, and there are only two other competitively produced goods. It is assumed that we always operate inside the capacity constraint, i.e. soda-water should be a free good, but is not. The advantages of this simple model (let us call it Second-Best and soda-water), besides saving algebra, are two. First, the problem that the monopolist uses too few resources is avoided, since he uses none. Second, the distortion (constraint) appears in a perfectly natural and tractable way: in order to maximize revenue, he wishes to set price (or quantity) so that the elasticity of demand for his product is -1. It is necessary, of course, to show that this can be written as a constraint in quantity space. I also show how the starting direction may be chosen, and how the algorithm works in this very simple model.

Readers of the important paper by Guesnerie and Laffont (1978) will realize that this model, in which First Best is desirable but unobtainable so long as the monopolist cannot be controlled, is an apparent counter-example to Corollary I (p. 437) of that paper. This Corollary states that, under certain conditions, appropriate taxes on the competitively produced goods will restore First Best even if the monopolist is immune from taxation (or other forms of control). The counter-example is, however, only apparent. Besides the obvious point that a First Best with free soda-water violates the regularity condition of positive consumer prices that is imposed by Guesnerie and Laffont, another more important difference between their model and this is that they permit lump-sum transfers, not only among consumers but between consumers and producers. The tax clerk programmed here may not indulge in any lump-sum transfers, and in fact is restricted to linear commodity taxes and subsidies which, in addition, must be chosen so as to balance his budget.[3]

That this very simple model may be extended to an arbitrary number of competitively produced goods, and even to a monopolist endowed with a regularly-behaved cost function, was shown in Archibald and Davidson (1983). For present illustrative purposes, and in view of the qualifications expressed above, I shall omit these generalizations here.

6.2   The model: a three-commodity economy

Let us consider a three-commodity economy, one commodity being what we shall call "soda-water," w – that is, the costless output of Cournot's mineral spring, run by an uncontrolled profit-maximizing monopolist. The other two commodities, x and y, are produced by firms competitive in both output and factor markets, according to a convex production possibility frontier

$$g(x, y) = 0. \tag{6.1}$$

(We may safely take it that the Second-Best solution requires that the economy satisfy the efficiency conditions in production since we have distortion in the commodity market only: see above. The economy is, of course, vertically integrated.)

It is convenient to write the monopolist's profit-maximizing price behavior as a constraint in the quantity space:

$$\eta(x, y, w) = 0. \tag{6.2}$$

That this can be done requires demonstration, which is more easily done when the notation is complete. It is necessary to assume that (6.2) is continuously differentiable. This is not here the innocuous assumption that it usually seems. Since the monopolist's profit function is not in general concave – again see Guesnerie and Laffont (1978) on this subject and previous literature cited there – the constraint $\eta = 0$ may well give a disconnected locus in quantity space. Our analysis will not be valid if the Second-Best optimum occurs, as it may, at a boundary point of one component of the locus, since marginal analysis will not be applicable there. It is assumed that the objective is to maximize a "representative" or aggregate utility function (say $u(x, y, w)$) of the produced commodities alone (see section 6.1 above). Maximization by consumers then requires that the marginal rates of substitution given by this function are to equal observed consumer price ratios.

If we denote producers' prices by qs and consumers' by ps, we can now justify the form of the constraint (6.2). For convenience, let us assume that our tax clerk fixes not the difference between the ps and the qs (whether taxes or subsidies, per unit or *ad valorem*), but the producer prices in the competitive sector. Thus our instruments are to be q_x and q_y, while the monopolist is free to choose p_w. The inverse demand for soda water may now be written as $p_w(q_x, q_y, w)$. Determination of the producer prices q_x and q_y means, however, determination of the quantities produced, x and y (from the production possibility frontier and the assumption of profit-maximizing behavior in the competitive sector). The demand function faced by the monopolist can thus be written simply as $p_w(x,y,w)$, and he chooses w to maximize $wp_w(x,y,w)$. This justifies writing the constraint imposed by his behavior as a constraint in quantity space, as in (6.2) above.[4]

The First-Best allocation in this problem is, of course, the allocation resulting from competitive markets for x and y and free distribution of soda-water. The presence of the uncontrolled monopolist means that only a Second-Best allocation can be achieved (there can be no tax-subsidy vector on the competitively produced goods such that a profit-maximizing monopolist will choose to give soda-water away). In general (Lipsey and Lancaster, 1957) this Second-Best allocation is not the same as that resulting from competitive markets for x and y. It is characterized by the first-order conditions:

$$u_x + \lambda g_x + \mu \eta_x = 0, \tag{6.3.1}$$
$$u_y + \lambda g_y + \mu \eta_y + 0, \tag{6.3.2}$$
$$u_w + \mu \eta_w = 0, \tag{6.3.3}$$
$$g = \eta = 0, \tag{6.3.4}$$

where λ and μ are Lagrange multipliers and subscripts denote partial derivatives. Equation (6.3.3) is justified by the fact that, although the monopolist cannot be directly controlled, we are here concerned with a "planning" problem. If we can impose taxes or subsidies on the competitive commodities x and y, it is clear that the Second-Best allocation can be reached, since any output (x, y) satisfying $g(x, y) = 0$ can be achieved by taxes/subsidies that yield the appropriate producer–price ratio.

Indeed, eliminating the multipliers from (6.3.3) we have

$$\frac{g_x}{g_y} = \frac{u_x - u_w \eta_x / \eta_w}{u_y - u_w \eta_y / \eta_w}$$

or, in terms of the prices,

$$\frac{q_x}{q_y} = \frac{p_x + p_w \left(\dfrac{\partial w}{\partial x} \right)}{p_y + p_w \left(\dfrac{\partial w}{\partial y} \right)}. \tag{6.4}$$

The second terms in the numerator and denominator of the right-hand side of (6.4) are the "corrections" (taxes and subsidies) to competitive prices that are needed to reach the Second-Best optimum. (Evidently the uncorrected competitive allocation is not, in general, the Second-Best allocation.) Certainly they cannot be computed directly without complete knowledge of the utility function and the two constraints. We shall see how they may be approximated without this knowledge.

The first problem is to tell the direction in which, from an arbitrary starting point such as the competitive allocation, the producer-price ratio should be changed to increase u, that is, to approach the Second-Best allocation. Consider the change in u induced by an infinitesimal movement along the production possibility frontier. It is

$$du = u_x dx + u_y dy + u_w dw$$
$$= m(p_x dx + p_y dy + p_w dw), \qquad (6.5)$$

where p_x, p_y, p_w are the consumer prices of the three commodities and m is the "marginal utility of income." In step-wise control we envisage only small changes, whence a differential formula such as (6.5) can be taken as a reasonable approximation. The "cost-benefit" criterion is marvellously simple: the tax clerk should proceed in whatever direction increases (real) GNE! In this simple case, we have

$$dy = -\frac{g_x}{g_y} dx$$

and, differentiating $\eta(x, y, w)$,

$$dw = \frac{(\eta_y g_x - \eta_x g_y)}{\eta_w g_y} dx$$

whence (6.5) becomes

$$du = m\, dx \left(p_x - \frac{g_x}{g_y} p_y + p_w \frac{\eta_y g_x - \eta_x g_y}{\eta_w g_y} \right). \qquad (6.6)$$

This can be rewritten as

$$du = mdx\left(p_x + p_y\frac{dy}{dx} + p_w\frac{dw}{dx}\right), \tag{6.7}$$

where the total derivatives dy/dx, dw/dx are the actual responses of the economy, subject to its constraints, to a tax/subsidy change that causes x to change by dx. (Remember that we have a one-dimensional choice problem here.) If the starting point is the competitive allocation, then $g_x/g_y = p_x/p_y$, and (6.7) is, at that point, just

$$du = mp_w dw. \tag{6.8}$$

The direction of change required is the direction that leads to increased sales of soda-water (which, since soda-water should be a free good but is not, is intuitively agreeable).

It is tempting to conclude here that one should, therefore, tax whichever of x and y is more of a substitute for w and subsidize the other. Often, of course, this will be true for almost any common definition of "substitute" (although see again the discussion in Lipsey and Lancaster, 1957). Here, however, the matter is somewhat different: whether the monopolist expands or contracts his output depends on the effect of the change on the *elasticity* of demand for his product, and this effect is not captured by any conventional definition. To *compute* such terms as η_x, η_y, we should need all the third derivatives of the utility function, but this computation is wholly unnecessary. In fact, we have the most empirically convenient result imaginable: the relevant derivative dw/dx is precisely the ratio of the observed changes in the two quantities, just what a clerk with only price and quantity information can most readily compute. Even when it is (6.7) rather than (6.8) that is appropriate (i.e. once step-wise control is under way) the other derivative dy/dx is again a ratio of observed changes. What we have, in effect, is Meade (make a small change) plus a criterion (cost-benefit) to tell us whether to repeat the dose or back off.

6.3 Comment on the model

The above is, of course, the simplest model we could devise. It remains to see how it might be generalized, and if any conclusions are warranted.

Extension of the number of goods in the competitive sector to some large n is largely a matter of notation (algebra) and adds no new insights. It does, however, reveal a most acute problem. If n is large, what initial tax-subsidy vector (or set of producers' prices) is the tax clerk to be instructed to try? The "trial space" for pure trial-and-error methods is obviously much too large. It seems unlikely that we can have adequate knowledge *in advance* of substitutability and complementarity as defined in section 6.2 above. The problem might be manageable if a reasonable number of well-behaved aggregates could be defined. Sufficient (not necessary) separability conditions for the existence of such aggregates were given in Archibald and Davidson (1983). It has since been shown, however (Blackorby, Davidson and Schworm, 1992) that the "representative consumer" itself depends on such extremely stringent separability conditons that the matter does not seem worth pursuing.

The alterations required if it is assumed that the production of soda-water does require resources (i.e. that the monopolist incurs positive marginal cost) are not profound: p_w in (6.7) and (6.8) above must be replaced by p_w minus marginal cost (suitably adjusted for the ratio of the consumer to the producer price of some numéraire commodity). Thus the violation of the usual regularity conditions on production in this model would be quite unimportant, were it not for the obvious difficulty in retrieving the required information on the monopolist's cost function.

There is no need to repeat the usual warnings about environmental stability and the relative speed of adjustment.

Little seems to be warranted by way of conclusion. Notice that, in addition to the limitations discussed in section 6.1 above, it has been assumed without discussion that the monopolist does not behave strategically. The most that can be said is that this chapter at least illustrates the possibility, at the general-equilibrium level, of making policy (parameter) changes by small steps, using the rear-vision mirror, if a suitable Criterion Function can be found. As has been noted above, the Criterion Function employed here has been chosen purely for simplicity and display. Any other criterion might be chosen, given that it has the property that the arguments of the function are easily observable during the process. What must be emphasized is that the choice for policy, rather than merely for display purposes, *cannot* be made without value judgments. (See again Blackorby and Donaldson, 1990.)

7

Two examples of the control process in a mixed economy

7.1 The class of problems considered

The purpose of ch. 7 is to illustrate two further uses of step-wise controls. Other examples might have been chosen. Thus an iterative control may be used to force a profit-maximizing multiproduct firm to Ramsay prices (see Finnsinger and Vogelsang, 1979). Ramsay prices themselves may require some justification, but after our consideration of the Rule may be thought of as at least having some plausible rationality. The iterative scheme proposed by Finnsinger and Vogelsang is, of course, informationally decentralized in the sense discussed in ch. 3; we need no information which is not obtained easily during the process. We have the usual trade-off between the possibilities of overshoot (lack of monotonicity) and strategic behavior.

Another attractive, but probably frustrating, example comes to mind: application to the control of a common-property, open-access, renewable resource such as a fishery. The target is obviously rent. Without control, open access ensures that this is dissipated in over-fishing. Most methods of control depend on constructing expensive, and usually unreliable, models of the fish population, and imposing quotas, restricting fishing methods, or both, incurring further resource cost, both for enforcement and for the required fishing methods (to say nothing of the problems of international agreement and enforcement on the high seas). Rent is then dissipated in all directions: it is certainly not collected. It would seem easy and natural to impose a tax on fish landed, and to endow the tax clerk with a simple little algorithm by which to adjust the rate until its yield was maximized. (We should know that rent was maximized since the open-access assumption ensures that the industry earns zero profit in equilibrium.) Unfortunately, it is very doubtful if relative adjustment speeds allow this simple solution. While we wait for an industry to reach equilibrium, relative prices, too, are likely to be changing (for example, that of fuel to the opportunity cost of fishermen). Worse, the environment is continually changing (pollution, water abstraction, and so on). And it is genuinely difficult to know how these changes are affecting stocks (probably well described by stochastic difference equations of appropriate order). One object of substituting an adaptive tax regime for present methods of control is to obviate the need to know; but it would require a great deal of faith to leave this matter entirely to the automatic pilot.

The two examples chosen here have some common features. In both cases, we shall consider the targets and managerial incentive structures for a single publically owned firm in an otherwise privately owned oligopoly. Thus we depart from Lerner's Problem, in which all firms outside the perfectly competitive sector are nationalized, and consider a problem not uncommon in many mixed economies in which, perhaps only by historical accident, a public corporation coexists (competes) with private firms. In both cases, the "industry" is sufficiently well defined for our purposes (by product homogeneity). Perhaps most interesting, in both cases it turns out that the behavior we want can be induced by making our manager's reward depend on *total* industry sales. In the first case, the target is, perhaps unfortunately, the Rule again; but it will be seen that the incentive and control system could be adapted to other targets. In the second case, the object is to remedy a market failure. The nature of this failure (in purely commercial TV broadcasting) is well known and has been much discussed. There is no suggestion of any "optimality" in the proposed cure, if only because costs are not analyzed. It may, however, seem in some sense "reasonable." It is the first example we shall encounter in which an iterative process is *not* required. The proposed incentive structure appears to leave no scope for strategic behavior, nor any need for policemen (abstracting from costs).

7.2 First example: the Harris–Wiens scheme (1980)

We consider here a case of a single public enterprise operating in an otherwise privately owned oligopoly. It is assumed that the product is homogeneous. (The examples which come most readily to my mind are unfortunately of non-renewable resources such as oil and minerals which cannot, of course, be properly dealt with in an essentially static framework.) Harris and Wiens (1980) take as their target obedience to the Rule, and propose an iterative control such that the single public enterprise can force marginal cost pricing upon the whole industry, retrieving the necessary information in the process. I shall not comment further on the Rule itself. Rather, I shall display the Harris–Wiens model preparatory to taking up the problem they neglected: choosing a reward function for the manager of the public enterprise such that it pays him to follow his instructions.

We have an industry, producing a homogeneous product, composed of $n+1$ firms with outputs $q_0, q_1, \ldots, q_n$, where q_0 is the output of the public enterprise. For convenience, write $Q = \sum_{i=o}^{n} q_i$. Assume that all firms can make a non-negative profit at the output at which marginal costs equals price. The public enterprise announces the reaction function

$$q_0 = Q^* - \sum_{i=1}^{n} q_i \tag{7.1}$$

where Q^* is optimal output (yet to be discovered). Now the profit of a private firm is given by

$$\Pi_i = q_i D\left(q_0 + \sum_{i=1}^{n} q_i\right) - C_i(q_i) \tag{7.2}$$

where $D(\cdot)$ is the inverse industry demand function and $C_i(q_i)$ is the cost function. Clearly Π_i is maximized by $\bar{q}_i$ such that

D

$D(Q^*) = C_i'(\bar{q}_i)$ and

$$q_0^* = Q^* - \sum_{i=1}^{n} \bar{q}_i. \tag{7.3}$$

(It is obviously assumed that $C_i''(q_i) > 0, \forall i$, over the relevant range. Recall our convention about stars and bars. The $\bar{q}_i$ of (7.3) may be understood to be starred as well.) It remains to find Q^* given the informational limitations assumed.

This is done by an iterative process. At each step the public enterprise announces a reaction function

$$q_0^t = Q^t - \sum_{i=1}^{n} q_i^t \tag{7.4}$$

where Q^t is the target at step t in the process. After the market has cleared, the target is revised according to

$$Q^{t+1} = \lambda\left(D(Q^t) - C_0'(q_0^t) \right)Q^t + Q^t \tag{7.5}$$

($\lambda > 0$). If, that is, the public enterprise finds that market price exceeds its marginal cost, it revises the target upwards. When $D(Q^t) - C_0'(q_0^t) = 0$ (or some small satisficing parameters), it knows, from the maximization of (7.2) by the profit-seeking private firms, that every producer's marginal costs are equal to the price.[1]

7.3   A solution: setting the incentive structure

We now have to set the incentive structure for the manager of the public enterprise. In solving Lerner's Problem (ch. 5) we used a variation of Domar's scheme: a bonus on profit together with a bonus on output. The innovation here, for the mixed-economy case, is that the bonus is to be paid on total industry output, not merely on own output. Thus consider the reward function,

$$R = \alpha + \beta(D(Q)q_0 - C_0(q_0)) + \gamma Q \quad \alpha \geq 0, \ \beta, \gamma > 0. \tag{7.6}$$

At any values of Q and q_0 this is decreasing in $C_0(q_0)$, as required. We have

$$\frac{\partial R}{\partial Q} = \beta \left(D'(Q)q_0 + D(Q)\frac{dq_0}{dQ} - C_0'(q_0)\frac{dq_0}{dQ} \right) + \gamma \qquad (7.7)$$

(suppressing superscripts on q_0 and Q). We wish to set γ and β such that the manager will wish to choose Q^* such that $D(Q) = C_0'(q_0)$. Using this, and setting (7.7) equal to zero, we see that we require

$$\frac{\gamma}{\beta} = -D'(Q)q_0 \qquad (7.8)$$

at the optimum (suppressing all stars and bars). This is the familiar result, with the slope of the industry's demand curve substituted for the slope of the public enterprise's demand curve.[2] Monitoring price and quantity during the iterative process in the usual way allows us to approximate (7.8) at least close to Q^* and q_0^*. We may easily check that $\partial E/\partial Q$ is positive to the left of Q^* and negative to the right, as required. With $Q < Q^*$, we have $dp_0/dQ > 0$ and $D(Q) - C_0'(q_0) > 0$ (from (7.5)), whence a sufficient condition for (7.7) to be positive is $\beta D'(Q)q_0 + \gamma \geq 0$. In the case of overshoot, the signs are reversed, and a sufficient condition is $\beta D'(Q)q_0 + \gamma \leq 0$. Conditions for uniqueness and convergence were discussed in ch. 5 (and see particularly Figure 5.1) in the case of a single monopolist. From (7.8) it is clear that the parallel condition here merely replaces $-f'(q)q$ with $-D'(Q)q_0$.

We can again go a little further in determining β and γ. Subject to satisfying the sign requirements, we wish β to be large: it is the incentive to cost minimize. At q_0^* profit may, however, be quite small (although positive by assumption). So we set γ large enough to drive the iterative process, and then set β, step by step during the iterative process, as large as (7.8) permits. If the resulting salary is "unreasonable" by some standard, we are free to adjust α.

The importance of cost minimization by the manager in this case derives not merely from our wish that the public enterprise itself be efficient. If the manager allows $C_0'(q_0)$ to be above its cost-minimizing value, he stops the iterative procedure too soon, with $Q < Q^*$ and price too high (see (7.5)). This is to the benefit of the private firms, who may offer the manager all sorts of inducements, from the promise of lucrative future employment to outright bribes. Indeed, I cannot see any way of guaranteeing that bribery will not pay (since padding $C_0'(q^0)$ by a dollar is likely to reduce $\beta\Pi_0$ by far less than it increases $\sum_{i=1}^{n} \Pi_i$). At least we have provided some reward for good behavior; and perhaps it should in any case be illegal for a public servant to resign in order to enter the employment of those with whom he was supposed to have dealt as a public servant. We may also take comfort in the fact that, if the pay-off to bribery is to be internalized, all the private firms must collude to negotiate and finance the bribe.

We have, nonetheless, to consider the possibility of strategic behavior. The Harris–Wiens adjustment coefficient is a constant, λ, not open to manipulation, and the stopping rule is immediate from (7.7). If we change the manager's reward function by predetermined steps, $\Delta\beta$, this is again exogenous to him (at the usual cost of not guaranteeing monotonicity). The alarming feature of this model is the small number of firms and the possibility of cooperative behavior. As long as (7.4) and (7.5) are strictly adhered to, and credible, it is not obvious what collusive behavior can achieve, apart from bribery and corruption. I cannot pretend, though, that I should feel entirely easy in my mind!

The object here is, of course, enforcement of the Rule, about which we may now have serious doubts. Clearly, though, the Harris–Wiens scheme, supplemented by the managerial incentive scheme, could be applied to other targets – if any simple ones can be justified.

7.4   Second example: TV programmes

If all TV channels are commercially operated for profit, and depend for their revenues on advertising, there is a clear possibility of market failure: reduplication of "popular" programmes (in the sense of high ratings) at some hours, and neglect of minority tastes. The "arithmetic" of this market failure was, to my knowledge, first pointed out by Steiner (1961), who also considered a cure. The possibility of market failure is very clearly taken into account in the *Peacock Report* on the Financing of the BBC (Peacock, 1986). The view expressed in that report is that the BBC and Channel 4 had, on the whole, operated in such a way as to preclude the market failure evident in the USA. The Committee concluded that this behavior was to be attributed to the methods of financing in use and, in particular, that the method should not be substantially changed (in particular, that the BBC should not take advertising), at least until potential major changes in technology were realized. In comparison, the point to be made here is a very small one. Not all countries, however, have institutions comparable to the BBC and IBA, whence, at least for countries in which commercial TV dominates, it may be worth exploring Steiner's proposed cure a little further.

Suppose (I take the liberty of further simplifying Steiner's already simple example) that, at some time, in some country or jurisdiction, there exist three commercial TV channels. Suppose further that, as profit maximizers, each of them wishes to choose the *type* of programme that will maximize its audience rating in order to attract advertising revenue. (This can obviously be only a *part* of an incompletely specified profit-maximizing problem: I do not now consider costs.) Suppose further that, at some specified time, more than 80% of the potential audience prefer a programme of type *A*, and the remainder one of type *B*. Simple arithmetic suggests that, in the search for advertising revenue, all three commercial channels, given non-cooperative behavior, will choose a type-*A* programme. Indeed, so long as the proportion of the potential audience preferring a type-*A* programme exceeds 0.8, the addition of a fourth channel, whether publicly owned or not, is "likely" to produce only a fourth type-*A* programme so long as the fourth channel is concerned only with *its* audience rating.

The cure Steiner suggested for this market failure was a publicly owned channel instructed to seek to maximize the *total audience* rather than its own individual rating. The problem I address here is the specification of a reward scheme for the manager of the publicly owned channel (enterprise) such that it will be in his own interest to make this his target, obviating the need for policemen. The target itself is admittedly arbitrary. It is, at best, only a partial solution to a partially specified problem since costs are entirely neglected. It must thus be assumed that we have set the manager's budget, or cost ceiling, on some other, and doubtless quite arbitrary, criterion, such as the revenue of an earmarked tax. The question posed is thus a limited one: if we wish to instruct the manager to behave in such a way as to maximize the total audience, what incentive can we give him to comply?

It seems immediately obvious that the answer, or part of it, must be to make the manager's reward depend on *total* audience ("industry sales"). This can be contrived to induce him to choose a type-B programme when the commercial choice would be type-A. Presumably we should, however, wish him to have some incentive directly related to the quality (here measurable only as popularity) of his own programme; and not to benefit, if it can be avoided, from exogenous changes (in tastes, or in the size of the potential audience). Some, at least, of these objectives may be reached by the following reward structure:

- Let N be the total potential audience.
- Let q be the proportion preferring a type-A programme at the specified time (for the moment, a fixed parameter).
- Let L be the number actually watching.
- Then $L = N$ or qN, depending on whether a type-B programme is or is not offered (on the somewhat extreme assumption that those who cannot have their preferred programme type do not watch at all).
- Let k be the number of commercial channels offering a type-A programme.
- Then the expected audience share for the public channel is $1/(k+1)$ if the manager offers a type-A programme and $1-q$ if he offers type-B.
- Define $s = 1/k(k+1)$ if he offers type-A and $s = 1-q$ if he offers type-B.

The manager's choice is assumed to be binary: A or B. Now we may write his reward function as

$$R(A) = \alpha + \beta q N + \gamma s q \tag{7.9}$$
$$R(B) = \alpha + \beta N + \gamma (1 - q). \tag{7.10}$$

Here in $R(A)$ the public channel's share, $s = 1/k(k+1)$, has been deflated, by k, from the expected value, $1/(k+1)$, since otherwise the manager will automatically choose A if $k=2$.

To set at least relative values of the parameter in (7.9) and (7.10), we use the condition, suggested above, that the manager should not benefit from an exogenous change in N, at least in the case that he has chosen B and all new watchers prefer A. Thus if $dN > 0$ and $d[(1-q)N] = 0$, we want $dR(B) = 0$. These two equalities give

$$dq = (1 - q)dN/N$$

and

$$\beta dN = \gamma dq.$$

Combining these two, we have

$$\beta = \gamma(1 - q)/N, \tag{7.11}$$

and, substituting into (7.9) and (7.10),

$$R(A) = \alpha + \gamma q(1 - q) + \gamma s q \tag{7.12}$$
$$R(B) = \alpha + 2\gamma(1 - q). \tag{7.13}$$

To remedy the market failure in the case described, we want $R(B) > R(A)$. Clearly $2\gamma(1-q) > \gamma q(1-q)$. The remaining term is $\gamma s q = \gamma q/k(k+1)$. For large k, this is small. In our example we have $q > 0.8$. Choose it to be 0.82. A little experiment will show that the critical value of s is approximately a quarter, which is exceeded by its expected value only if $k = 1$.

This seems to "work," at least by the scanty criteria proposed here. In the limiting case $k = 1$, we might even prefer a second type-A programme in the interests of variety and competition in quality, but these criteria have not been seriously introduced. Let us check the other features of the reward scheme of (7.12) and (7.13). $R(A)$ is increasing in q, $R(B)$ decreasing. This may be reasonable. q has been treated as exogenous, and the manager should not be rewarded or punished for an exogenous change in tastes (unless it is to signal a switch between A and B). If there is some endogeneity in q, the manager has an appropriate incentive to try to increase it (presumably by trying to improve the "quality" of his type-B programme). It might appear that an exogenous increase in $\mathcal{N}$ would increase $R(B)$, but setting $\beta\gamma$ as in (7.11) avoids this. It is, however, true that an exogenous increase in $\mathcal{N}$, all new watchers preferring type-B, increases $R(B)$ by $\gamma d\mathcal{N}/\mathcal{N}$. And it is not possible to distinguish between exogenous and induced changes in q.

Information appears to present no difficulty, which is why an iterative process is not required. From (7.12) and (7.13), it is seen that only $s(=1/k(k+1))$ and q need be known, not even $\mathcal{N}$. s must be an obvious matter of common knowledge. For q it seems necessary to rely on ordinary audience ratings. The parameters in the reward functions are constrained by (7.11). Subject to that, they may be set at whatever levels seem likely to generate a competitive, opportunity-cost, salary for the manager.

The result is that Steiner's (1961) suggestion for government intervention to redress a case of market failure is feasible. We can instruct the manager of the public channel appropriately, and ensure incentive compatibility. Information requirements are trivial. To say anything non-trivial about costs, the determination of the budget of the public channel, or quality is, however, quite another matter, beyond the scope of this volume. Reading Peacock (1986), one might think that, given the existence of an institution such as the BBC, the practical problem is not to find a manager willing to do his job – this sort of incentive system appears to be unnecessary. The practical problems are, first, to determine his budget (a social choice problem) and, second, to give him suitable cost incentives. These I have not discussed. The future technology envisaged by Peacock would mean that the viewing could be priced on a pay-per-view or a pay-per-channel basis. Then it might be possible to define the "profit" of the publicly owned channels, and give managers the sort of incentive discussed earlier.

Part III

Non-convexities

8

Non-convexities in the technology

8.1   The Second Theorem reconsidered

As the assumptions of the model have been altered, the Second Theorem may so far have appeared quite robust. It survives the introduction of extended preferences if they are assumed to satisfy the non-paternalist condition. Introduction of effort-aversion certainly destroys the optimality of the simple Rule, but not by automatic implication the Theorem: there is no obvious reason why it should not survive in a properly constructed model (which I do not provide). Introduction of risk is another matter; we lose not only the Rule but, in the absence of complete and costless information, the possibility of attaining First Best at all. It remains to consider increasing returns to scale, which, in the consideration of Lerner's Problem (ch. 5), I was careful to postpone. A sufficient reason was that a partial-equilibrium framework is inadequate to the treatment of this problem. The important result, which requires general-equilibrium analysis, is that, in the presence of non-convexities, the "divorce," seemingly justified by the Second Theorem, between considerations of efficiency and of distribution, or equity, cannot be made. There is, of course, quite another reason for thinking this divorce impossible (which will not be further explored here). If the simple notion of the representative consumer cannot be employed (see again Blackorby, Davidson, and Schworm, 1991), then any Criterion Function employed to judge any change must aggregate preferences in a fashion that must depend on value judgments. (The apparent exceptions to this – actual, as opposed to potential Pareto-improvements – are discussed in Part IV below.)

It follows that subsidies to "decreasing-cost" industries, proposed by Pigou (1920) as well as Lerner, would require much more serious justification than they have had, or can have in partial-equilibrium models that necessarily ignore distribution. Even the "escape" by two-part tariffs (in those cases in which they are feasible, i.e. resale is impracticable) proves to entail startling information requirements.

These results have been established by Guesnerie (1975), followed by Brown and Heal (1979) and (1980), whence in this chapter I shall only give a brief and heuristic account. In ch. 9, I shall give reason to think that "increasingness of returns" may be a phenomenon not confined to public utilities and a few major production processes, but instead be almost ubiquitous.

8.2 A non-convex technology

Consider the production possibility frontier (ppf) drawn for a two-good economy in Figure 8.1, where leisure is ignored, and both industries display some increasingness. Suppose that there is a tangency between the ppf and a Scitovsky community indifference curve at A. This indifference curve lies below B which is, accordingly, Pareto-superior to A. It is, however, well known that the Scitovsky curves may cross. If we move to B, with the distributional changes entailed by the change in resource prices, we may well find a tangency with a Scitovsky curve there, and this curve may somewhere cross the curve tangent at A. Indeed, as drawn, it lies below A, whence A is Pareto-superior to B. This economy does not have an efficient equilibrium. (There may well be a tangency with a member of another family of Scitovsky curves in the region of C; and the equilibrium here *may* be Pareto-inferior to A *and* B!) It follows at once that the criterion "potential Pareto-improvements" may not induce a transitive ordering of social states.

It now emerges that we must be more careful in our description of an "economy." This is usually provided by the values of $(X, \gtrsim, Y, \omega)$ where X is the set of consumption sets, $\gtrsim$ of

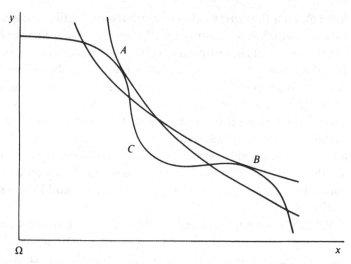

Figure 8.1   A non-convex ppf

orderings, Υ the set of production possibilities, and ω the initial endowment. The economy we have just illustrated in Figure 8.1 does not have an efficient equilibrium. We may consider "equivalent" economies, equivalent in the sense that only the allocation of the initial endowment between individual agents is changed. Thus the description has to be enlarged by specifying the complete individual endowment, ω_i. Then it has been shown that, in general, there exists, among the set of equivalent economies, at least one ω_i ($\hat{\omega}_i$, say) such that an efficient equilibrium does exist. It is also true that efficiency then requires the equality of the MRSs with the MRTs in the usual manner, which implies that decreasing-costs industries must make losses.

To assist intuition, recall that, in the economy of Figure 8.1, A is Pareto-superior to B, and B to A. This contradiction suggests that both are inside the utility possibility frontier for this class of equivalent economies; and so they are. Brown and Heal (1979) construct this frontier for a two-agent economy and a piece-wise linear but non-convex ppf. The analogous points, A' and B', say, are both within the frontier, as might be expected. This in turn suggests that some scheme of lump-sum tax and subsidy ("unrequited transfers," as Brown and Heal put it) might lead to an ω_i such that there exists a solution on the utility possibility frontier (which is necessarily an efficient solution). That at least one such ω_i exists in any class of equivalent economies is proved. It is of some interest that equal endowments usually give such an ω_i. One may recall the analogous result in the discussion of "envy-free" economies (ch. 2). I shall not, however, pursue the matter since these are economies without the complication of variable factor supplies. When the supply of labor is variable, and agents are heterogenous as inputs, then we encounter quite another class of difficulties in reconciling efficiency and equity which I do not take up here (but see Archibald and Donaldson, 1979).

What we have then is that, if the technology is non-convex, efficiency cannot only not be considered independently of distribution, but depends on it. We also have that, at an efficient equilibrium, decreasing-cost industries make losses. These losses must somehow be paid for, and in a manner consistent with the maintenance of ω_i. Two suggestions have been offered. Suppose first that ω_i is achieved by equal initial allocations: every agent has an equal share in every firm. To make him pay his share of the losses, the decreasing-cost industries are nationalized, as with Lerner, and he pays his share of losses in his role as taxpayer. This may be attractive. (The problem of managerial efficiency in such a case was discussed in ch. 5.) Alternatively, we rely on two-part tariffs. This, of course, is feasible only if resale is impracticable, as it generally is in the case of public utilities. We shall, however, see below that the phenomenon of increasing returns is unlikely to be so conveniently restricted. Furthermore, the standing part of the tariff must be tailored to the individual, or "personalized": the arbitrary imposition of standing charges may well conflict with ω_i. This requires information about the tastes of individual agents which, even if attainable, would itself be costly.

This chapter is deliberately brief. Its purpose is to recall some important results published by others to serve as introduction to ch. 9.

9

Non-convexity and optimal product choice

9.1 Product choice

It is my purpose here to suggest that increasingness, with the attendant impossibility of divorcing considerations of efficiency and of equity, is a much more common phenomenon than is sometimes thought. I start with what may appear to be a digression.

How many models of automobile should be produced? To maximize welfare under some resource constraint, how many brands of soap powder or styles of shirt are required? How well, indeed, are we equipped to answer such questions? The honest answer to the last question must, I think, be "poorly." We may *guess* that planned economics have done a bad job of product selection. We may *guess* that capitalist economies have done better, although the record is much obscured by non-competitive structures and practices. We have no serious criteria to determine what would be the optimal product set in an ideal economy, whether planned or not. Yet distinct and differentiated products clearly claim a non-trivial proportion of economic activity, at least in more affluent economies.

There seem to be two obstacles to our progress. The first is easily overcome, and has been, by adopting a convenient theoretical approach. The second, as we shall see, is the impossibility of disentangling efficiency and equity in dealing with the problem.

9.2 The characteristics approach

A full-dress "justification" of the characteristics approach is, at this date, surely otiose; and, indeed, the literature is now too ample to be cited in full.[1] Nonetheless, a few brief remarks may be appropriate.

If we follow the tradition of Walras and Hicks, we have a given set of goods, finite or at least countable. Consumer preferences, and the technology, must be defined over this set. It is then quite difficult to handle a change in the vector of goods actually produced, the introduction, let us say, of a new good. We seem to have a choice. We may say that the list of goods has changed, the technological possibilities have changed, and consumer preferences are to be redefinied over the new list of goods. In this case, there appears to be no possibility of saying anything about the welfare implications of the new good. Alternatively, we may affirm that the new good was all the time in the complete list of possible goods, of which the subset actually produced has changed. Then, however, the list of all possible goods belongs in some Platonic space of ideal forms, to which the technological possibilities and the preferences also belong. It is not clear that this approach offers much help.

It does seem very much simpler and more straightforward to adopt the characteristics of goods, rather than the goods themselves, as our primitives. It is necessary to assume, of course, that the list of characteristics on which consumer preferences are defined is, if not immutable, at least much less prone to change than the vector of goods actually produced at any time. On this, there is, as yet, sadly little empirical evidence, but it seems at least intuitively plausible, whence I shall make this assumption. Consumer preferences and the technology are accordingly defined on characteristics. For expositional convenience, I shall also assume the existence of a subset of characteristics (for the moment, only two) with properties described as follows.

(1) The consumer's utility function, defined on characteristics, $\mathbf{z}$, and written $\phi(z_1, z_2, \ldots, z_i, \ldots, z_m)$ is weakly separable, that is, can be written $U(\mathbf{z}) = u[h(z_1, z_2), z_3, \ldots, z_m]$. I shall make standard assumptions on the form of this function below.

(2) The effect of any changes in prices or factor demand in the production of goods embodying z_1 and z_2 is so widely diffused as to be negligible, and thus to occasion no significant feed-back.

The consequence of these two assumptions is that we can conduct partial-equilibrium analysis in the space of $z_1 - z_2$, where I assume that the consumer's no-worse-than sets are convex in the usual manner. (Concern about the aggregation of preferences may be postponed for the moment.)

It is now desirable to describe the technology in the space of $z_1 - z_2$. I assume, and shall continue to assume, that it is continuous: a good embodying z_1 and z_2 in any *ratio* can be produced. A produced good may be described by a vector from the origin, with length given by some resource use or price yet to be described. For some good y_i, say, let the angle between this vector and the z_1-axis be θ_i. The ratio between the characteristics is then given by $\tan \theta_i$ (see Figure 9.1). Continuity means that if a good described by θ_i can be produced, so can a good described by $\theta_i + \varepsilon$, ε as small as we care to make it. (It may, in fact, not be possible to produce a good such that $\theta = 0$ or $\theta = 90°$, although possible to produce a good ε – close to each axis. This difficulty need not concern us for the moment.)

Now, suppose that in addition to continuity, we assumed (i) constant returns to scale and (ii) a constant rate of transformation in production between the two characteristics, yielding the frontier (for, say, one dollar's worth of resources) labelled LL′ in Figure 9.1. I wish to argue that, while either or both of these assumptions might be true in some cases, neither can be true in the general case of interest.

Assumption (i), CRS

Let preferences be diverse, in the sense that there are many tangencies between LL′ and the indifference curves of individual agents. (We could obviously go on to define a continuum of preferences in an obvious sense; but all that matters here is that there be some diversity.) Now, if there are *any* transactions costs associated with buying the goods or any costs of transport or of combining pairs of goods to achieve a more preferred θ, there

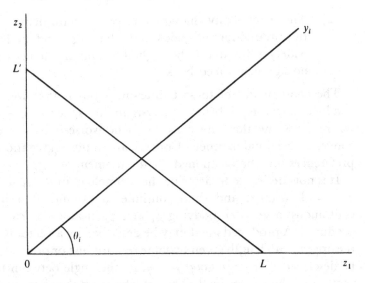

Figure 9.1   A good in characteristics-space

will be as many "production points" (goods) as there are "consumption points" (in the limit, a continuum). If there are no such costs, only two production points are needed, one at each end, at $\theta = 0$ and at $\theta = 90°$ (or, if this is not precisely possible, as close as may be). Diverse preferences will be accommodated by diverse combinations of the two goods. Thus in a space of two characteristics, either only two goods will be produced or very many (in the limit, an uncountable infinity). Neither of these two polar cases can be reconciled with common observation of the markets for many consumer goods. It therefore appears that we must assume at least some increasingness of returns. There may then be more goods than characteristics, but how many more remains to be determined.

Assumption (ii), constant MRT between characteristics in production

This is a factual matter, about which we have very little information, at least in a readily retrievable form. I can say only that it seems grossly unreasonable to me, and give illustrations. It is well known that it is impossible to design automobiles which, for constant outlay, can be made to go faster and faster without giving up more and more of other desirable characteristics (fuel economy, say, or leg room, or braking ability). This is a consequence of physical laws of which there must be innumerable analogous examples, such as the lightness and rigidity of a bicycle frame, or the lightness and warmth of clothing. I shall therefore assume decreasing MRT between characteristics in production.

9.3 The technology and the ppf

It might seem that discussion could now be terminated. If the reasons given in section 9.2 above for rejecting CRS are valid, we may simply recall ch. 8, and, arguing that increasingness is not confined to public utility cases (in which resale is, or can be made, impossible, and appropriate two-part tariffs can at least be designed, if not implemented), conclude that the divorce between efficiency and distribution cannot be granted for, at least, any developed economy of interest. There is, however, something more. I wish to show that even a well-informed and benevolent planner could not make decisions about what goods to produce without consideration for the distribution of welfare.

To proceed, we must be able to construct some sort of possibility frontier in the $z_1 - z_2$ space. With CRS, any arbitrary normalization will do. With some increasingness, this is not true. We can, however, make either of two assumptions which will make the construction possible and, I hope, plausible. Recall the assumptions made in section 9.2 above to justify partial-equilibrium analysis: separability in preferences and only negligible feed-back between this sector and others. It follows that, if we assume that an initial equilibrium exists, factor prices are given, and we may work in terms of cost functions. We may make either of two assumptions: (a) for any good described by θ_i, the long-run average cost curve is U-shaped; (b) it is J-shaped in the fashion described by Bain (1954). In both cases there is a well defined minimum efficient scale, or MES. In case (a), of course, a sufficiently large demand would require replication of plant specific to θ_1, in case (b) merely expansion; but this need

not concern us now. Given the existence of the MES, we may
normalize on that output to construct the ppf illustrated in
Figure 9.2. It is a locus of possibilities and is, by assumption,
continuous. (As noticed above, it may not actually intercept the
axes, but this, too, need not concern us now.)

Now, how many and which goods on this ppf will be, or
should be, produced? Let us start with the positive question, to
which, indeed, a wholly satisfactory answer cannot be given.
Recall that an economy may be described by $(X_i, \gtrsim, Y, \omega)$. We
have now considerably specialized our assumptions about X_i,
$\gtrsim$, and Y. Nonetheless, the answer must depend on (1)
preferences, the initial endowment and its distribution, the
actual scale at which MES is reached, *and* (2) what assumptions
are made about cooperative behavior among producers, the
possibility of pre-emptive entry in an expanding market, and
the like. Let us ignore difficulties associated with (2). This is a
non-trivial, indeed a heroic, assumption. Note that, in two-
space, a good can have no more than two neighbors! "Ignoring
the difficulties" really amounts to making two assumptions:
first, that each firm produces only one good (in one plant –
spatial problems are entirely ignored), and, second, that
behavior is both non-cooperative and non-predatory. Assume
that demand is quantitatively sufficient, relative to MES, and
sufficiently diverse, that a finite subset of the possible goods is
actually produced, as shown in section 9.2 above. I assume,
largely for convenience (to ensure that the market frontier
offered to consumers is itself convex), that the goods may be
freely combined by consumers to yield the most preferred values
of θ. A "sample" of indifference curves is illustrated in Figure
9.2.

Before considering the planner's problem, we must consider
one more technological problem. Is fixed capital θ-specific, or
does it have "scope" (over θ)? This is another empirical question
on which the evidence, though it doubtless exists, is hard to
retrieve. There is illustrative, or anecdotal, evidence aplenty. A
lathe, never mind a hammer, may be used on a wide variety of
products. The equipment designed to produce four-cylinder
engines cannot be converted overnight to the production of

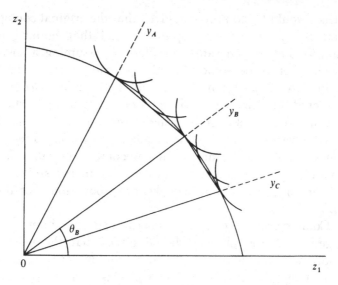

Figure 9.2   Preferences, and a locus of possibilities

six-cylinder engines. An aircraft may go anywhere there is an adequate landing ground, a railroad track is where it is laid. And so on. What, for our purposes, is it best to assume? I shall adopt what I think is a neutral, compromising, minimal assumption: any plant producing a good described by θ_i uses enough equipment specific to θ_i that a change to some θ_j, even if θ_i and θ_j are in some sense "close," entails some capital expenditure and hence a deliberate decision.

9.4   Failure of the Second Theorem

What, now, is the planner's problem? Starting from the situation in Figure 9.2, he cannot be faced with the "empty plain" problem. This is deliberate. If the list of relevant characteristics (those on which utility functions are defined) is historically stable, as it is convenient to suppose, the empty plain experiment simply does not occur. I prefer to follow Eaton and Lipsey (1980) in assuming that θ-specific capital wears out a bit at a time, so that the problem is one of replacement. This, indeed, would be no problem, given that the original configuration was in any sense "optimal," and that nothing had changed. Let us generate a problem by assuming a specific change. Let it be some capital equipment specific to the production of y_B that has worn out. Let our knowledgeable planner also be aware that, since that equipment was installed, there has been a change in tastes: some mass of demand has shifted towards z_2. Thus many people whose preferred mix was θ_B or a mix of y_B and y_C now want a mix of y_B and y_A: there is less demand for y_C. Let us assume, however, that there is still enough demand for y_C to justify its being kept in production at or above MES.

"Common sense," or some sort of rule of thumb, immediately suggests that the planner should direct that the worn-out θ_B-specific equipment be replaced by equipment suitable to a product more z_2-intensive than θ_B. This, indeed, is what is required by rules derived from the aggregate consumers' surplus criterion. Notice, however, that there are, by assumption, still some consumers who prefer the original characteristics mix: θ_B, or a more z_1-intensive mix, obtained by combining y_B with y_C. The welfare of these consumers will obviously be reduced if y_B is replaced by a product more z_2-intensive. One may, of course, draw more diagrams, and purport to "measure" their loss, but the fact still is that the planner's decision depends upon his weighing of the gains of one subset of consumers against the losses of another. This is a clearly a distributive matter. Replacing the step-wise, one-plant-at-a-time, experiment described here with some other, such as the empty plain experiment, will not alter that.

It is clear that, if there is any association between income and preferred θ, a change in income distribution, without any change in any individual preferences, will present the planner with the same problem.

If the decision of an omniscient and benevolent planner depends upon distributive criteria, so must any "welfare" criterion. The leading candidate is, of course, aggregate consumers' surplus. This criterion will justify the planner in deciding on a more z_2-intensive product. Spence (1976) uses the surplus criterion in his analysis of monopolistic competition in the conventional goods-space. Even aggregating in this manner he is unable to say more than that monopolistic competition may lead to the production of too few goods – or too many. Yet it seems that he has exploited the model and the technique he chooses as thoroughly as possible.

At this point one might reasonably wonder if the distributive consequences of product choice are of any quantitative importance. Suppose that the distribution of the initial endowment were satisfactory, should any reasonable observer *care* if shirt styles are not exactly to everyone's taste? I do not offer any measure of utilities, but there are reasons for thinking that the matter is not to be easily dismissed.

First, at least in an affluent society, a very large proportion of our expenditure is on differentiated, or branded, products. I have no quantitative estimates, but the reader is invited to consider his expenditures on housing, appliances, furniture, automobiles, entertainment, and so on. It might be thought that the aggregate welfare losses, in some loose and undefined sense, would be non-trivial if minority tastes were not catered for, presumably larger if, for some reason, minority tastes were allowed to dictate, and larger again if the planner was neither benevolent nor well informed.

Second, there are serious difficulties in computing "real incomes." The initial endowments cannot, of course, be valued until a set of prices is known. What is more difficult is that the vector of products actually produced now has to be known. If we wish to evaluate changes in real incomes, we have not merely the usual index number problem, but the additional problem of accounting for changes in the vector of goods produced. An index of the shadow prices of the characteristics themselves would obviously be helpful. Gorman (1980/1956) has shown how the shadow prices may themselves be computed. The construction of an index itself waits, of course, upon the identification of relevant characteristics and the necessary data retrieval.[2]

9.5   What if economies of scale are exhausted?

It will have been noticed that, in our discussion of the planner's problem in section 9.4 above, the need to cover the losses of increasing returns' industries under marginal-cost pricing has not even been mentioned. From the assumption that demand is sufficient to support the output of each produced good at, or above, MES, it follows that there are no losses (at MES, of course, long-run average and marginal costs are equal). Clearly we could alter demand, or the vector of goods produced so that, at marginal-cost prices, some or all goods produced did make losses, but this is not much to the point. The point is that the fact of non-convexity, of some increasingness, forces a choice of goods to produce, even if the economies of scale for those produced *are* exhausted. Thus non-convexity is itself sufficient to prohibit the disassociation of efficiency and distribution, whether or not there are losses which directly entail distributional considerations. Most of the literature is concerned with these losses, and overlooks the fact that, even if there are none, efficiency and equity considerations cannot be divorced. This result is in no sense an artifact or accidental consequence of adopting characteristics as our primitives of analysis: recall that, if returns and the MRT between characteristics were constant, we could span the two-space with two goods (and analogously in higher dimensional spaces); and if the MRT were not constant, or there were any costs to combining goods, then with CRS we could produce whatever number of goods the diversity of tastes called for (in the limit, a continuum).

9.6   Possible asymptotic properties of monopolistic competition

We may say, then, that the need to allocate the losses occasioned by producing a good at a quantity such that economies of scale are not exhausted is an aggravation of the problem, not *the* problem of non-convexity and the Second Theorem. Two questions naturally occur: (i) is there an MES for every good? and (ii) in what circumstances might output be on at least that scale for all, or even most, goods?

The mere fact of scarcity would seem to require a qualified "yes" to (i). It is qualified because a counter-example is familiar. Thus suppose that it took a "large" capital outlay to open up Cournot's mineral spring, after which variable costs were zero up to some virtually unlimited capacity. I shall show below that this possibility, if indeed it is one, is of little importance.

(ii) invites us to consider the asymptotic properties of the model. Can we expect economies of scale to be exhausted, so that the economy is effectively convexified, if only the economy is "large" enough (in some sense to be defined)?

The asymptotic properties of a model of monopolistic competition have been thoroughly studied by Hart (1979). He adopts goods rather than characteristics as his primitives, and makes two assumptions which seem to "force" his conclusion (that monopolistic competition is asymptotically competitive).[3] The first is that the output of each firm is bounded from above. The second is that preferences can be represented by a fixed and finite list. This in turn means that the economy "grows" by replication: the incomes of existing consumers may be increased, or the number of consumers. It does not matter which, since a new consumer can be only a clone of a previously existing one. The vector of possible goods is fixed and finite. It follows that, by replication, we can make the demand for each of them as large as we please. With the output of each firm bounded from above (but the factor endowment growing in proportion to consumer demand) we can make the number of firms producing each good as large as we please. The result – that even if the market is initially monopolistic, it is asymptotically competitive – follows naturally.

As to how these results may translate to a model in characteristics-space I can, at present, offer only a conjecture. It is, I hope, a plausible conjecture, but I have as yet no proof. As well as translating to characteristics-space, it is desirable to alter the two of Hart's assumptions singled out above. Consider first how preferences may behave as the economy grows without limit. It seems to me that diversity of preferences is a fairly conspicuous human characteristic, a diversity which gains strength as the budget set expands. Thus I do not think that we should restrict ourselves to the cloning of preferences that Hart assumes. An advantage of taking characteristics instead of goods as our primitives is that it is easy to drop this restriction. We have only to think of the increasing occurrence of points of tangency of individual indifference curves with the frontier illustrated in Figure 9.2. In the limit, of course, these points will form a continuum, and we may speak of a "continuum of preferences": goods described by every value of θ are in demand. Furthermore, by continuing to increase numbers and incomes without limit, we can make the mass of demand on any interval of the frontier as large as we please, and the interval as small as we please.

It is this last argument that makes it seem less hazardous to replace Hart's assumption that each firm's output is bounded from above with the MES assumption made here. The interval, say $\theta_i + \varepsilon, \theta_i - \varepsilon$, around any produced θ_i becomes smaller and smaller; and the mass of demand in that interval larger and larger. In this case, the distinction between a MES attributable to U-shaped long-run average cost curves and one attributable to Bain's curves becomes less important than may have first appeared. In the former case, we may have replication of plants specialized to some θ_i, or merely products "very close" in θ. In the latter case, replication is not necessary, but we may also "pack" the products (firms) as close as we please. In either case, two assumptions are still difficult: the assumption of "one-firm-one-product," and the assumption of non-cooperative non-predatory behavior.

Now not even the overhead costs of Cournot's mineral spring occasion any difficulty. The capacity constraint must be finite; and, more important, any finite fixed cost can be covered by a price as close to marginal cost (or zero) as we like if quantity demanded grows without limit.

It is conjectured then that, in the limit, monopolistic competition is competitive.[4] More immediately important, short of that limit, the welfare problem of product choice consequent upon even "a little" increasingness remains, even if outputs of the chosen products occasion no losses.

Part IV

Cooperatives

10

Pareto-improvements and cooperatives

10.1 Pareto-improvements and the prisoners' dilemma

Adaptive control systems may have some desirable properties, particularly in comparison with planning systems, but First Best is clearly unattainable, simple rules derived from it cannot be relied upon and, it seems, the divorce between efficiency and distribution cannot be granted. An immediate question, then, is what scope, if any, is left for applied welfare economics. My concern in this book is with implementation. Is there anything left to implement? An obvious answer is that there still may be cases in which Pareto-improvements are possible; and that we may look for such cases, and suggest, if possible, means to attain the improvements. There is a school of thought which maintains that possibilities of improvement – the attainment even of what we may call "local" efficiency – are all about us, but are commonly blocked by ignorance and prejudice: unenlightened self-interest, in fact. I fear that I do not believe it. Such schools tend to rely overmuch on *potential*, rather than *actual*, compensation, relying, it would seem, on the notion that anything that could be done may be regarded as being as good as done. In cases in which distribution is ignored, or left "to the market," potential losers are neither ignorant nor unenlightened if they resist change, although they are doubtless self-interested. Free trade is a case in point. It is simply not true that all agents always benefit from a move towards freer trade. Yet there remains a school of economists that would have us think that objections even to discriminating local customs unions are based only on unenlightened self-interest, for which the proper remedy is more "information." It is also desirable to remember what has long been known: the criterion "potential Pareto-improvement" may well induce an intransitive ordering of possible social states. (The shortcomings of the potential Pareto criterion, and of the sum of Hicksian compensating variations, for use in applied welfare economics are discussed in a review article, to my mind definitive, by Blackorby and Donaldson, 1990.)

I wish to consider here some cases in which Pareto-improvement does seem feasible, but the obstacle is both more serious and more tractable than pigheaded ignorance or sheer bloody-mindedness. These are cases, generally speaking, of the prisoners' dilemma, writ large, or of the analogous free-rider problem. If in such cases we can design appropriate institutions (which here will not require adaptive controls), then we can rely on self-interest to achieve the improvement. To be "appropriate," of course, an institution (perhaps a surrogate market) must generate the information required by agents and provide an effective incentive scheme: it must, that is, economize on both love and policemen.

10.2 Labor-managed firms and the range of markets

I shall consider in some detail only two examples in Part IV, both concerned with producers' cooperatives or labor-managed firms (henceforth for brevity LMFs). There seem to be several good reasons for addressing oneself to the possible problems of an LMF, or indeed an economy of LMFs (henceforth for brevity ELMF, a pedestrian alterative to Ward's "Illyria"). Such an economy was seriously proposed, on grounds both of equity and efficiency, by J.S. Mill (1848), but in his discussion of efficiency he did not advance far beyond a serious critique of the incentive structure within a capitalist firm. The possibility of an ELMF was then largely ignored by professional economists until the publication of Ward's classic (1958) paper. From his model, Ward derived the famous and perplexing "perverse supply curve": it appeared that an LMF would wish to respond to a reduction in product price by an increase in output and vice versa. An ELMF would not be viable in the face of such behavior by its component LMFs. Fortunately, this perversity disappeared when Miyazaki and Neary (1983) showed that a voluntary association of utility-maximizing individuals could make far more satisfactory arrangements for short-run income smoothing in the face of price variability. This leaves us free to consider other matters.

Clearly, an ELMF operating, so far as possible, in competitive markets, is an alternative to both competitive capitalism and public ownership with central planning. It is, of course, necessary to avoid the temptation to compare an ideal form of one system with a realization of another, whence I shall try to avoid example, and, indeed, any sort of empirical observation. Comparison, even of ideal types, is, however, difficult even in pure theory, as we shall see. The advantages of an ELMF over competitive capitalism were supposed by Mill to lie in distributional equity and the incentive structure within the individual firm. I shall have nothing more to say about distribution, but the free-rider problem within any LMF requires serious attention (see ch. 11). Further, a well known difficulty with models of competitive capitalism is that of an incomplete set of markets. Clearly we may encounter the same difficulty with an ELMF. Indeed, for that reason, and for the reasons discussed in Part III above, the attainment of First Best in any of these systems seems to be quite out of reach. If it were attainable in one and only one of the three systems then, distributional considerations aside, the argument would be over. Similarly, if it were attainable in all, comparison would depend solely on distributional considerations. As it is, no such general or overall comparison is possible. We can proceed only in a piecemeal manner, making such suggestions for local Pareto-improvements within the ideal type of a system as may occur to us. I shall in fact concern myself in Part IV only with an ELMF, for two reasons: first, we probably know more already about an ideal type of competitive capitalism, which may in some cases provide a useful guide or standard; and, second, some difficulties inherent in at least Lerner's alternative to planning in an economy in which capital is publicly owned have already been discussed at length.

If inadequacy of the set of markets is a problem for models of competitive capitalism, it is likely that it also is for models of an ELMF. We must therefore pay special attention to risk-sharing in an ELMF. This is done in ch. 12, but there is much of concern that is not dealt with there, and can be mentioned here only in a somewhat cursory manner. There appears to be a school of thought, enthusiastic advocates of an ideal "cooperation," who ignore the warning that we must examine even the ideal type of a system for incentive compatibility, and seek, in the design of any scheme, to economize on love. Advocates of ideal "cooperation," in this sense, deliberately plan to restrict the range of markets. The matter has been admirably discussed by Barzelay and Thomas (1986) and need not be rehearsed at length here. It is also appropriate to notice here the work of Dow (1986). Dow demonstrates analytically the equivalence of the LMF and capitalist ownership *in perfect competiton*. "Perfect competiton" must here be understood to include full and costless information and the absence of risk. Dow concludes that any difference between the two systems, in allocation and efficiency, must be explained in terms of imperfections of competition. Two imperfections, in this broad sense, that would occasion difficulty to the LMF are addressed in chs. 11 and 12. (It is worth remarking that these three papers – Miyazaki and Neary, 1983, Barzelay and Thomas, 1986, and Dow, 1986 – permit us to neglect any detailed comment on the rest of the large body of literature that has followed Ward, 1958.) First, let us consider one example of an imperfection consequent upon inadequate markets that might seriously impede an LMF.

The example is concerned with investment by an LMF. If investment is to be financed by retained earnings, or by mortgaging, in some sense, future earnings (and how else can it be financed?), then its desirability to the individual member must depend on his age if his income on retirement is independent of the future earning power of his LMF. Indeed, in this extreme case, the investment plan that pays him best is one that allows the capital to collapse the day after he retires! Clearly, if the LMF is to have anything of the "immortality" of the joint-stock company, its members must have a financial interest in its future. To insist, however, that an individual's retirement income depend solely on the future income of his LMF is to deny him the opportunity of diversifying his portfolio: it is to require him to put all his eggs into one basket, his non-human assets into the same basket as his human capital.[1]

Precisely how this paradox is to be resolved, I do not know, but the general outline of a qualitative solution is clear enough. We wish the individual member to have an interest in the present value of his LMF on his retirement. This is attained if he is the owner of some marketable share. There are those who would rule this out on the grounds that it is contrary to some essential "spirit of cooperation." One may suggest, in turn, that ownership of voting shares might be confined to working members, while other shareholders would have no vote, or a vote on only some matters. If, however, the individual member is to have a reasonably diversified portfolio, he must be allowed, if not encouraged, to acquire other assets besides some doubtless small share in the LMF in which he works. This might be accomplished by, for example, requiring each LMF to establish and maintain a properly vested pension trust fund to which each member might contribute. Diversification requires, however, that the pension fund shall not lend substantially to its own LMF – it might, in fact, be allowed to hold no shares, or only some small proportion. But then there must be other assets that it can hold. This in turn suggests that it be able to hold shares (perhaps non-voting shares) in other LMFs, or at least in financial intermediaries who lend to other LMFs, perhaps acting as "mutual funds" or "unit trusts."

I am not proposing to write a code of company law for an ELMF. The point of the foregoing is that we should be thinking of extending the set of markets in an ELMF, not of restricting it.

10.3 Ownership in labor-managed firms

One point in section 10.2 above requires further comment. How are the active members of an LMF to acquire shares, other than by the accident of "vesting day" or by squatters' rights? More generally, how do new members of the labor force obtain entry to any LMF, and what is to be done if for any reason (change in technology, or in tastes) the membership is found to be excessive? These are really general-equilibrium questions, having to do with the allocation of labor, and its mobility, and seem to be rather neglected in the literature on the LMF, at least as far as I have read. I cannot pretend to answer all these questions, but offer a few suggestions.

Membership of a successful LMF has some of the attributes of membership of a good club. It might therefore be thought appropriate that membership should be paid for, particularly if members are to become shareholders. Perhaps a mortgage scheme for the purchase of voting shares by working members could be designed. Clearly, though, if members are not to be "locked in," these shares *must* be transferable: this is a necessary condition for labor mobility. How the individual LMF decides on and arranges long-run expansion or contraction of membership remains a little mysterious. Some "sensible" results might be obtained from the assumption of present-value maximization, in conjunction with transferability of shares, in place of maximization of static net revenue or expected utility. I have not yet explored this possibility. (But see again Dow, 1986. Dow's model is not really dynamic in the required sense, e.g. members' ages are not considered.)

10.4   Innovation in labor-managed firms

There are many other questions concerning the desirable structure of an ELMF which will not be explored in chs. 11 and 12. I shall content myself with a final example. A virtue of capitalism is generally held to be its ability to adapt, and particularly to innovate: indeed, Marx pointed out the historical record of success. Grafting product innovation, at least, onto an ideal model of *competitive* capitalism is, however, not easy, and, given the problems of product choice (see ch. 9), may be impossible.[2] Who is to be responsible for experiment and risky innovation in a planned economy is similarly obscure. Matters are no better in a model of an ideal, competitive, ELMF.

The ELMF may indeed be superior in its ability to adapt to one sort of innovation: labor-saving technological change.

Suppose that a labor-saving innovation is available to an LMF (which is certainly vague, since who might develop it, and for what reward, remain mysterious). Suppose further that the elasticity of demand is such that its net effect, after allowing for increased output, will be to save labor. (This, as stated, is inconsistent with the assumption that the LMF sells in a perfect market but note that it is always possible to twist the isoquants in such a way that the outcome is net labor-saving.) The LMF can adopt the innovation with enthusiasm. Each member can enjoy some combination of increased income and reduced effort. The latter may be taken in the form of shorter hours, longer vacations, or earlier retirement, as desired. There is, in any case, no conflict of interest between owners and workers, no reason for quarrels over redundancy, or any attempt at "feather-bedding." Compensation is actual rather than potential (see section 10.1 above). The objection is not to the operation of enlightened self-interest (which might well lead to attempted feather-bedding in a capitalist economy), but rather to a purely distributional issue: why should the lucky members of *this* LMF receive all the rewards? A partial answer, at least, is that, *if* the ELMF is competitive, the rewards will prove to be only quasi-rents. (Other sources of rent, and possible methods of taxing rents, in an ELMF as well as a capitalist economy, are discussed in the Appendix, pp. 149–154.)

10.5 Labor-managed firms and unions

Mention of feather-bedding in section 10.4 above suggests the remaining question about the structure of an ELMF that I shall venture to discuss: unions. There is no place for unions in ideal competitive capitalism (see Simons, 1944), and presumably not in an ELMF either. If the workers are the shareholders, what could a union be *for*? Evidently there is no role for a union in matters of wages. It is, however, well known that unions have another function, that of attending, in their members' interests, to what is sometimes called "industrial jurisprudence." It might be thought that the cooperative structure itself renders this function otiose. Yet we have been warned that the tyranny of the majority can be as odious as any other, in particular that of overbearing and unregulated foremen. One might thus be tempted to think that unions do have a function in an ELMF. Yet a union, as well as an LMF, is governed by majority rule and may be tyrannous. This suggests that the LMF should be subject to some code of law. Laws, unfortunately, require enforcement (policemen). I must leave the matter there. (I return in ch. 12 to the desirability of the members of an LMF having at least similar tastes.)

11

Achieving Pareto-efficiency in the LMF[1]

11.1 Cooperative and free-rider solutions

In ch. 11 I shall discuss possible solutions to a well known problem: how may an LMF escape the prisoners' dilemma and achieve the cooperative instead of the free-rider solution? The difficulty is obvious. Members are rewarded by shares in the net product. Assume (for the moment) what is not essential, that the shares are equal. Also assume what is vital, that these shares exhaust the product. Then the member who "shirks" or free-rides saves his own effort while losing only $1/N$th of this marginal product (in an N-member LMF). The temptation is obvious. Indeed, "honest" members, aware of the possibility, and unable to trust their colleagues, may well feel trapped: who can wish to be a "Stakhanovite sucker" in a world of free-riders? It is not enough to depend on goodwill or some "cooperative spirit." It is only prudent to assume that most agents are, most of the time, ordinary selfish maximizers, and to design structures (incentive schemes) which accommodate this. It follows that we must somehow provide for contracts or agreements on levels of effort and reward which will be efficient *and* for an incentive (or enforcement) arrangement such that it pays to honor them, so that each member in turn can expect his colleagues to honor their own: the cooperative solution. I shall consider here some possible ways of doing this. Let us first set out the assumed structure of our LMF and characterize its efficiency conditions.

11.2   The model: members of the LMF

Assume that the LMF has a fixed number of members, N, indexed by i. (The assumption of a given, fixed, membership may appear arbitrary, and indeed it is. We may in the end obtain some insight into the matter of appropriate membership size.) Each member has preferences over income, y_i, and effort, e_i, that are represented by a differentiable and strictly quasi-concave utility function $U^i(y_i,e_i), U^i_1 > 0$ and $U^i_2 < 0, \forall i \varepsilon N$. Each member supplies effort from a compact set $[0, \bar{e}_i]$, and any vector of effort inputs $\mathbf{e}$ lies in the Cartesian N-fold product, X, of these sets. The technology is represented by a differentiable and strictly quasi-concave production function $f(\mathbf{e})$. (We can for the immediate purpose neglect fixed costs without any loss of generality.) For any $\mathbf{e}$ in X assume that $f_i(\mathbf{e}) = \partial f(\mathbf{e}) / \partial e_i > 0, \forall i \varepsilon N$: no member or subset of members is indispensable in the sense that positive output is achieved even without their effort. Finally, since output is bounded above by $\bar{f} = f(\bar{\mathbf{e}})$, individual incomes must lie in the compact set $[0, \bar{f}]$. (We normalize the output price at unity.)

The associated maximization problem for the LMF is familiar. It is to find a $2N$-tuple $(\mathbf{y}^*, \mathbf{e}^*)$ that solves

$$\max_{(\mathbf{y},\mathbf{e})} \sum_{i \varepsilon N} \alpha_i U^i(y_i, e_i)$$

$$\text{subject to } f(\mathbf{e}) - \sum_i y_i \geq 0 \qquad (11.1)$$

where the weights α satisfy $\alpha_i \varepsilon [0,1]$ and $\Sigma_i \alpha_i = 1$. The weights, of course, "drop out" from first-order conditions, but we may notice that there is no law of God or cooperative behavior that requires them to be equal: the LMF can, if it wishes, perfectly well give higher weights to the utilities of members perceived to be more highly skilled or merely more senior.

The first-order conditions for (11.1) are, of course,

$$U^i_1(y^*_i, e^*_i) / U^i_2(y^*_i, e^*_i) = -1 / f_i(\mathbf{e}^*), \forall i \varepsilon N$$

and   (11.2)

$$f(\mathbf{e}^*) - \sum_{i \varepsilon N} y^*_i = 0.$$

These are the necessary conditions for Pareto-efficiency. The assumptions already made on the forms of $U^i(\cdot)$ and $f(\cdot)$ ensure that sufficient second-order conditions are satisfied wherever (11.2) is. The set of efficient outcomes defined by (11.2) is large. Let us write it as $E = \{\mathbf{y}^*, \mathbf{e}^* | U^* \text{ is Pareto-efficient}\}$.

Assume that the LMF initially operates at a feasible but inefficient status quo vector $(\mathbf{y}^0, \mathbf{e}^0)$, yielding the utilities $\mathbf{U}^0$. This may be the free-rider outcome. The set of Pareto-dominant outcomes may be written $F^0 = \{\mathbf{y}, \mathbf{e} | U \geq U^0\}$. We may define the contract set as $C = E \cap F^0$.

As a preliminary step, we may imagine a game in which members bid for themselves feasible income–effort combinations, and show that the Nash-equilibria of this game are in the contract set. I call this a "preliminary" step because we have yet to provide any arrangement that makes the cooperative solution enforceable, and consequently credible to each member, and because it is necessary to endow each member with more information than I consider plausible. Preferences are assumed to be private information, whence no member can know the limits of the utility possibility set. This assumption will be adhered to. For the moment, it is also necessary to assume that each member knows the technological limits, that is, $f(\cdot)$, an assumption further discussed in section 11.5 below. The set of income–effort vectors that are strictly feasible is defined as

$$A\{\mathbf{y}, \mathbf{e} | f(\mathbf{e}) - \sum_i y_i = 0\}.$$ The "rules of the game" specify that

each member specifies ("bids") an income–effort pair $\hat{y}_i, \hat{e}_i$, with pay-offs

$$
\begin{aligned}
U^i &= U^i(\hat{y}_i, \hat{e}_i) \text{ if } (\hat{y}, \hat{e}) \in A \\
U^i &= U^i(y_i^0, e_i^0) \text{ if } (\hat{y}, \hat{e}) \notin A.
\end{aligned}
\tag{11.3}
$$

That is, individual members receive their bid-pairs only if the entire vector of bids is feasible; if not, it is ruled that agreement has not been reached, and the status quo obtains. This structure allows each member to veto an outcome that would provide less than the status quo utility, while forcing him to make a bid that is feasible given the bids of other members, provided that there is a utility-increasing bid open.

The Nash-equilibria of this game may now be characterized. For any vector of other members' bids, $(\hat{\mathbf{y}}_{-i}, \hat{\mathbf{e}}_{-i})$, the ith member will choose a bid to

$$\max_{y_i, e_i} U_i(y_i, e_i) \text{ subject to } y_i = f(e_i, \hat{\mathbf{e}}_{-1}) - \sum_{j \neq i} \hat{y}_j, \quad (11.4)$$

where the constraint follows from the pay-off structure described in (11.3). An interior solution to (11.4) must satisfy the efficiency conditions given in (11.2), that is

$$U_1^i(\hat{y}_i, \hat{e}_i) / U_2^i(\hat{y}_i, \hat{e}_i) = -1/f_i(\mathbf{e}). \quad (11.5)$$

Thus a Nash-equilibrium to this game is an income–effort vector that solves (11.4) for each member, is feasible, and provides increased utility for each member. It is accordingly in the contract set C. The assumed concavity of $f(\cdot)$ is sufficient for existence of such an equilibrium.

11.3 Incentives and Holmstrom's scheme (1982)

It may be encouraging to know that a Nash-equilibrium here yields the cooperative, or Pareto-efficient, solution, but we have still provided no arrangement for arriving at it, or any plausible enforcement mechanism. Let us first consider the incentive structure of an LMF, and then possible mechanisms by which the members can reach an agreement.

It is customary in the literature on effort and incentives to distinguish two polar cases, effort unobservable and observable. The world is rarely so simply described as either zero or one: we usually expect an intermediate case in which effort can be observed, with more or less accuracy, at some cost. Nonetheless it will be convenient to confine ouselves here to the polar case, effort unobservable, for two reasons. The first is simple: an incentive scheme sufficiently robust to handle the zero case will certainly handle intermediate cases. The second is more subtle. There may be good reason for trying to arrange matters so that effort need not be observed in the LMF even if it can be. If it can be observed, we must immediately ask: by whom? An LMF could, of course, hire monitors (supervisors, foremen) to undertake the same work of monitoring and policing that they are supposed to do in the capitalist firm of Alchian and Demsetz (1972). This must seem a sad outcome, particularly to those who think cooperation a social arrangement morally preferable to capitalism for purposes of production. It also rules out what has often been regarded as a chief method by which an LMF may save costs compared to its capitalist counterpart. The obvious alternative is that members monitor each other, which they may presumably do with no or little cost as each goes about his or her own work. It is not, however, obvious that people would much care to work in an environment in which everyone is to watch his fellow worker, look over his shoulder, time his absences in the washroom . . . The "company" monitor might be preferred, being perceived as a common enemy. I accordingly confine myself to the zero case: effort is unobservable, whether because that is indeed true, or because an incentive structure such that it need not be observed is to be preferred in any case.

Now the force of Holmstrom's (1982) work is that any agreement, including one satisfying the efficiency conditions of (11.2) above, is subject to the free-rider problem if individual income is given by output shares, as in (11.1), and the budget is to be balanced (product exhausted) as in (11.2). Holmstrom suggests an incentive scheme which potentially "breaks the budget." If the agreed upon effort, $\hat{\mathbf{e}}$, let us say (since this scheme is not confined to the case $\hat{\mathbf{e}} = \mathbf{e}^*$) is delivered, each member gets his share of the corresponding $\hat{\mathbf{y}}$; and if it is not, he gets nothing. "Nothing" is in fact unnecessarily drastic: we may be able to choose some non-negative low or punitive wage k. Choice of k is, unfortunately not easy. We want k such that $U^i(k,0)$ is less than $U^i(y_i^0, e_i^0)$. We cannot, of course, compare (unobservable) effort with that at the status quo; and, of course, preferences are private information. Probably all we can do is set k to be little, if any, larger than a member's income if unemployed. Then Holmstrom's reward scheme can be written

$$
\begin{aligned}
y_i &= \hat{y}_i & &\text{if} & f(\mathbf{e}) &= f(\hat{\mathbf{e}}) \\
y_i &= \min\{k, f(\cdot)/N\} & &\text{if} & f(\mathbf{e}) &< f(\hat{\mathbf{e}})
\end{aligned}
\tag{11.6}
$$

with the surplus to be shared by some rule, say the weights α of (11.1), if $f(e) > f(\hat{e})$. (The "min" is required to guard against the possibility that kN actually exceeds realized output.) A standard interpretation of this rule is that each worker receives a (low) minimum wage, but a bonus if an agreed target is achieved. It is necessary to show that, at least in the case $\hat{e} = e^*$, deviation from the agreement cannot pay any member or coalition of members, but there is another point to consider first.

The scheme described by (11.6) may seem morally distasteful: collective responsibility and punishment[2] in a case in which, by assumption, no individual can observe his fellow's action, much less control it, and so cannot reasonably be held responsible for it. This difficulty is easily overcome. Imagine (what is certainly not the case) that it were well established that capital punishment were a 100 percent deterrent to murder: one might not have much moral hesitation about voting for it! This scheme also respects the individual's endowment constraint. Whatever happens, his income is positive. He is not to be fined. (There is no point in proposing a scheme which can simply be frustrated by individual bankruptcy.)

It might seem obvious from (11.6) that free-riding does not pay, but, for an agreement to be made, *and adhered to*, it must be credible to all members that (11.6) is enforceable. Since it requires potential budget-breaking rather than income-sharing, credibility depends on there being an enforcement scheme. This depends on what is to happen to the surplus if some member (or members) were to misbehave, so that the punitive clause of (11.6) were invoked.

11.4   Trustworthy third parties

Holmstrom (1982) suggested that the surplus could be collected by the shareholders of a capitalist firm (by paying a minimum wage without an output bonus) whereas a cooperative would have no way of breaking the budget, and would therefore be unable to adopt such an incentive structure. Archibald and Neary (1983), followed by MacLeod (1987), suggested that, even in the LMF, a third party, or "sink" for a potential surplus can be found. Suppose that the production process is separable in subsets of labor inputs, so that we may write

$$f(\mathbf{e}) = h(\mathbf{e}_H, g(\mathbf{e}_G)) \tag{11.7}$$

where $H = \mathcal{N} - G$, $\mathbf{e}_H, \mathbf{e}_G$ are the corresponding input vectors, and $\partial h(\cdot)/\partial g > 0$. Examples come readily to mind of a sequence of activities in (for example) assembly-shop, paint-shop, and packing-shop. If the production function can be written in the form of equation (11.7), then there are subfirm units (distinct teams) characterized by technological unity and distinct, measurable, contributions to final output. In the 1970s literature on Yugoslavian cooperatives each was known as a BOAL (Basic Organization of Associated Labour): see Horvat (1976). The suggestion was that BOALs within the firm could serve as third parties or "sinks" for each other, instead of shareholders. The BOALs would thus contract with each other for agreed effort and target output, and misbehavior in one (failure to reach its agreed target) would lead to appropriation of the surplus (11.6) by the other.

Before we ask where a plausible third party may be found if the production process is not separable, there is another awkward question, seemingly overlooked in this literature so far. It may pay members, or a subset of members, of one BOAL to bribe a subset of members of another (which subset might, indeed, have only one element) to default on purpose, thus creating a surplus. This raises the *quis custodiet* question again; and again see Eswaran and Kotwal (1984). Somehow, then, a "trustworthy sink" must be found, external to the firm, as it must be if the production function is not separable, if, that is, the members of the LMF cannot conveniently be divided into teams of BOALs.

Where should we look for a trustworthy third party, and, preferably, one who is in any case well informed about the LMF? I suggest a financial intermediary, henceforth known simply as the "bank." As fixed costs have been ignored in this chapter, there has been no role for the bank, whose main functions appear only in ch. 12, where risk-sharing in the ELMF is discussed. Our immediate problem is, however, to ensure that the bank is a trustworthy sink which, if it is a profit-sharing cooperative, it may not be, any more than another BOAL. Here I can only follow the suggestion made by Eaton and White (1983): bank officers are to be considered as being in "positions of trust," and, to regulate their behavior without merely running into the individual bankruptcy constraint, are to be paid a salary sufficiently in excess of their opportunity cost that mere dismissal is a serious deterrent penalty.

We now have a credible scheme for enforcing a contract in the form of (11.6), but are we entitled to call it a "contract" at all? MacLeod (1987) (and see also his 1988) points out that while output is observable and effort is not, explicit contracts can be made about the former (whether with another team or with the bank), only "implicit" contracts or arrangements about the latter, presumably between the members of the same team. Let us make sure that, if (11.6) is backed up by a credible enforcement mechanism (a "trustworthy sink"), it does not pay a member of a team (or coalition of members) to cheat. If they do, they get, at best, $U^i(k,0)$ which is intended to be less than any pay-off they need voluntarily agree on. Those who do not cheat, of course, do worse, getting, at best, $U^i(k,\hat{e}_i)$, (using again $\hat{}$ to denote agreed values) whence the incentive to cheat is always stronger if one thinks that others will, i.e. that (11.6) is not a credible deterrent. What cheaters cannot rely on is that fellow members, wanting to realize the incomes $\hat{y}_i$, will work harder to "take up the slack": with effort unobservable they do not know that anyone is shirking until output is realized. Thus to attempt this sort of blackmail, cheaters would have to announce their intention. This would presumably entail their identification and, while I still do not wish to propose a code of laws for the ELMF, it seems that this announcement might well lead to expulsion.

11.5   An auction process

If we think that this adaptation of Holmstrom's budget-breaking scheme solves the incentive problem for the LMF, we still have to provide some mechanism by which the members can come to an agreement. We must also remember the point made by MacLeod (1987 and 1988)[3] that $\mathbf{e}^*$, not being observable, cannot be made the subject of any explicit contract. "Agreement" is therefore better described as agreement to an implicit contract; but it seems desirable that individual commitments e_i^* be voluntarily agreed on and be public knowledge to all members. Some possible ways of reaching agreement have been suggested. As we know, if we treat the agreement process as a one-shot game, its Nash-equilibria are in the contract set (vectors $(\mathbf{y}^*, \mathbf{e}^*)$). This, however, does not help us to specify a mechanism. MacLeod has suggested that, given enforcement, learning, particularly in a repeated game, will elicit the cooperative solution. Archibald and Neary (1983) suggested an auction or *tâtonnement* process in which each member bids income–effort pairs to arrive at an agreement. It is this last suggestion that I shall explore further here.

Before describing the *tâtonnement* process, let us reconsider the state of each agent's information.

(1) Preferences are private. This entails, in particular, that no one can know the utility possibility frontier.

(2) Each member knows that the rule described in (11.6) is in force and enforceable. This implies that he can reasonably expect any voluntary commitment to be honored.

(3) In section 11.2 above, it was assumed that each member was sufficiently informed on the properties of $f(\cdot)$ to calculate his pay-off matrix. This assumption is required by any game theoretic treatment of the problem. I should prefer to assume at least initial ignorance of $f(\cdot)$.

Now for the auctioneer. He may be thought of as "our" agent but, perhaps better, as a manager already chosen by the LMF. Like Walras' auctioneer, he cannot know in advance what equilibrium values will be. He must, however, have some information and some rules. (1) and (2) above certainly hold for him. While he cannot be entirely ignorant of $f(\cdot)$, it would be hopelessly inconsistent with earlier parts of this book, particularly ch. 4, to endow him with full qualitative and quantitative knowledge of $f(\cdot)$ *ab initio*. Realistically, the most he probably has is an approximation built up from the limited domain of experience (probably of interior, free-rider solutions). For the moment, we may endow him with at least a workable approximation. Later, we may wish to allow him some learning process. It will clearly be helpful if his rules satisfy the properties that Malinvaud (1967) required of a good planning procedure (see ch. 3). This is difficult because of the members' ignorance (above) and because no restrictions have yet been imposed on bidding strategies.

Let us consider two possible stopping rules.

(1)   The auctioneer may arbitrarily stop the process at any round t, and announce at the beginning that he will stop at discretion. This rule would induce utility-increasing bids: indeed, the prudent agent would follow a maximin strategy. It neither guarantees feasibility, nor rules out an interior solution.

(2)   If the auctioneer calculates that a vector of bids has converged to a point (at least approximately) on the frontier, he always calls for a last round ("Going, going, . . .") so that members may at least make a last utility-increasing bid if it is open to them.

These possibilities serve only to reveal more problems. (a) What is the auctioneer to do if, for some bid vector $(\mathbf{y}^t, \mathbf{e}^t)$, $f(\mathbf{e}^t) - \Sigma y_i^t \neq 0$? And (b) Why should there be a convergent sequence if no restrictions are placed on bidding strategies?

(a)   Suppose first that the frontier has not been reached, and that there is an undistributed surplus. The auctioneer has only to distribute this, according to any weights, and announce the adjusted vector $(\hat{\mathbf{y}}^{t+1}, \hat{\mathbf{e}}^{t+1})$ as the new status quo.

Suppose now that the members' claims more than exhaust the product, so that $f(\mathbf{e}^t) - \Sigma y_i^t < 0$. The auctioneer may generate a final feasible bid vector by taking a convex combination of this vector and the last bid vector (which could not have been outside the frontier, or this procedure would have already been in use). Thus he announces the bids

$$\hat{e}_i^{t+1} = s^t \hat{e}_i^t + (1 - s^t)\hat{e}_i^{t-1}$$
$$\hat{y}_i^{t+1} = s^t \hat{y}_i^t + (1 - s^t)\hat{y}_i^{t-1}$$

where $s = \varepsilon(0,1)$ is a scalar chosen to satisfy

$$G(s^t) = f\left\{(s^t\hat{e}^t + (1 - s^t)\hat{e}^{t-1}\right\} - \left\{\sum_i (s^t\hat{y}_i^t + (1 - s^t)\hat{y}_i^{t-1}\right\} = 0.$$
(11.8)

We may be sure that an s satisfying (11.8) exists since, by construction, $G(0) = 0$ and $G(1) < 0$, and it can be shown that $G'(0)$ is positive.

Notice that both of these adjustments are left to the auctioneer. It is clear that he must know the limits of the feasible set (see section 11.6 below). It is hard to suppose that members do, at least initially but, if they do not, the application of the auctioneer's adjustment rules will inform them.

(b)   There is no reason to think that a convergent sequence of bids exists unless some restriction is put upon bidding strategies, yet bidding strategies should be endogenous, chosen by the agents in the circumstances in which they are placed. If we restricted all members to Cournot–Nash behavior we should, of course, have no problem. This seems to be arbitrary, but might be easier to justify in the context of a repeated game with learning and (11.6) in force. Neary and I (1983) suggested what seems a milder restriction. That is that each member's bid is based on a k-element subset of previous bids, $B^t = \{(\mathbf{y}^{t-r}, \mathbf{e}^{t-r})\}_{r=1}^k$, so that his bidding rule can be represented by *continuous functions*:

$$Y_i: B^t \to [0, \bar{f}]$$
$$L_i: B^t \to [0, \bar{e}_i] \qquad \forall i.$$
(11.9)

This unfortunately seems to require that each member know $\bar{f}$, contrary to what was assumed above. We can overcome this difficulty by requiring that the k-element of B^t be bids registered by the auctioneer *after* any necessary adjustment under the rules given in (a) above.

Now we may formulate our stopping rule and demonstrate both convergence and efficiency. The process is to stop if a vector of bids at $t-1$ is feasible *and repeated* at t. This is the "Going, going . . ." rule that always allows a member a "last chance" to make a utility-increasing bid if he can see one (and which, if not feasible, will be adjusted).

The assumption of continuity in (11.9), together with continuity in the auctioneer's adjustment rules under (a), give us convergence. Each of the infinite sequence of bid vectors (y_i^t, e_i^t) with origin $(\mathbf{y}^0, \mathbf{e}^0)$ lies in the compact set $[0, \bar{e}_i] \times [0, \bar{f}]$, whence there must be a subset of indices t such that the corresponding $\mathcal{N}$ subsequences converge simultaneously. We have already established feasibility (by the auctioneer's adjustment rules). Efficiency follows from the fact that, if there were a better outcome available to any member given the utilities of others then, under the stopping rule, he could have claimed it: given self-interest, the *tâtonnement* will not stop at any point that is Pareto-dominated. Thus the outcome of the *tâtonnement* process is, like a Nash-equilibrium, in the contract set.

11.6 Information problems

It is individually rational for the member to vote for the apparently Draconian rules of (11.6) if he knows that he has only to commit himself *voluntarily* to a level of effort (and income). Vice versa, it is rational so to commit oneself if one knows that (11.6) is in place, whence other members can be expected to honor their commitments. The commitments may be reached as the outcome of a cooperative game, a repeated game with learning, or a *tâtonnement* of the sort just described (which may be regarded as a non-cooperative game in extensive form). There is still a serious information problem.

Who knows, or can know, what the limits of the physically feasible set are? I have put the onus on the auctioneer, or manager here, and he may indeed find out (improve his approximation) by trial and error (repeated *tâtonnement* and consequent physical experiment). It is the errors that are troublesome, given (11.6). Overfulfillment of the target (on agreed y^*) can be dealt with easily: an unexpected bonus for each member. But suppose that achieved output is less than y^*. It is not obvious that anyone, members, manager, or the bank, can distinguish between possible causes: lack of information (over-optimism about the feasible set) or shirking. It would be nice to imagine that the bank were a sympathetic as well as a trustworthy sink, and would believe the manager when he explained that it was his fault – if he could, in fact, know! And if (11.6) is not enforced, even "once," will it again be credible? Apart from noting once again the value of information, I do not know what more to say.

11.7 Limits of partial equilibrium

We started with an arbitrary production function $f(\cdot)$ and an arbitrary number of members $\mathcal{N}$ with unknown preferences. Suppose now that (y^*, e^*) are agreed upon and achieved. Given diminishing returns, this membership may be too many or too few (or too greedy or too effort-averse) for long-run viability (and, indeed, an arbitrarily constructed LMF need not be viable at all). As we have already noticed, problems of the general equilibrium allocation of labor in an ELMF have scarcely been explored. Presumably if this LMF has too many members (given other opportunities) some will leave. If it has too few, it "should" recruit more, but how it is to be required to share its "luck" with others I do not know, and shall not consider here.

12

Risk-sharing in Illyria (or the ELMF)[1]

12.1 Risk and moral hazard

It was noticed in ch. 10 that, in thinking about an ideal type of ELMF, it is desirable to think of extending, rather than shrinking, the set of markets. This is particularly evident when we introduce risk.[2] Ideally, a risk-averse LMF would perhaps bear no risk, a solution rendered impossible by the familiar problem of moral hazard. *This* moral hazard is quite distinct from that encountered in ch. 11. Indeed, I shall now assume that the LMF of ch. 11 does, normally and regularly, achieve the cooperative solution to its internal (riskless) problem. Given that assumption it is, I think, only a harmless simplification to take the next step, and assume that all the members have identical utility functions. There remain the simultaneous problems of risk-sharing between the LMF and some other agency and the incentive to effort. The question is, does there exist an incentive-compatible (Second-Best) risk-sharing contract into which both sides may rationally enter?

To see the difficulty, let us introduce risk to Ward's classic (1958) model without making any other amendment. In this model, workers are to choose membership n and capital k to maximize a member's income y_i where

$$y_i = \frac{1}{n}\{pg(k,n) - rk\}, \tag{12.1}$$

$g(\cdot)$ is the (neo-classical) production function and r an exogenously determined interest rate. There are several possible interpretations of the financial structure (ownership of the capital; determination of r) which will be discussed below, but let us for the moment consider the standard case: the capital is "owned" by the state (or a state owned financial intermediary, henceforth simply called the bank) which lends it at a fixed rate r. Now risk is introduced by making p a (positive) random variable. If no change is made in the financial structure, then if the bank is risk-neutral and the workers are risk-averse, this is the pessimum risk-sharing arrangement; it amounts to 100 percent bond finance, with the workers bearing all the risk. The workers would obviously prefer to be guaranteed a wage equal to $E[y]$ in 12.1 above, leaving the bank to bear all the risk (r a residual, or 100 percent equity finance). Even the assumption that the members reach the cooperative solution does not free this solution from moral hazard. Thus replace the production function $g(\cdot)$ in (12.1) with $h(k,n,e)$, increasing in all its arguments and otherwise "properly behaved" (but with a variation in notation from ch. 11: e is now total effort supplied). Now the expectation of y_i is conditional on the supply of effort, some target or agreed $\bar{e}$. If each worker is now guaranteed his expected share of $E[y|\bar{e}]$, the moral hazard problem is immediate.

Obstacles to observation or monitoring were discussed in section 11.3 above. The obvious alternative is coinsurance or risk-sharing, which I shall discuss here.

12.2 Risk-sharing

We have to distinguish between two possible cases, which I call the *ex ante* and *ex post* cases. In both, the contract between LMF and bank must be settled before the state of nature is known. In the *ex ante* case effort must be committed – work done – before the state of nature is known. In the *ex post* case effort is committed only when the state of nature is known.[3] One obvious difference between the two cases may be noticed at once: in the *ex ante* case workers will "almost always" regret *ex post* their choice of effort, whereas in the *ex post* case they need never regret it. Intended supply is thus completely inelastic with respect to product price in the *ex ante* case, whereas in the *ex post* case it is not. The *ex ante* case appears to be rather the more general and more interesting; and, once it is solved, the *ex post* case is very easy. I shall accordingly confine myself here to the *ex ante* case, and leave the *ex post* case to Appendix B to ch. 12.

The state of nature will henceforth be interpreted as simply the product price, p in (12.1) above. There are many other random elements contributing to revenue, such as weather, machine breakdown, and supply failure. Further, the LMF may not sell in a perfectly competitive market but still face stochastic demand. For these reasons, an appropriately general model would employ a revenue function $R = R(x;k,n,e)$ where x is a random variable corresponding to the state of nature. The multiplicative case is analytically more tractable (cf. Leland, 1972), and will be employed here. I do not believe that, for present purposes, this entails any loss of generality, provided that one proviso is borne in mind: although I shall convention-ally call the multiplicative random variable in the revenue function the price, I do not wish to assume in the *ex ante* case that the bank can costlessly decompose any realized revenue into price and output (uniquely reflecting effort, since it is assumed that n and k are known), any more than it could in the more general case. Indeed, I shall assume that the bank is as limited in its information as it would be in that case, although it must, of course, know the distribution of net revenue. Thus I do not consider the "forcing contracts" discussed by Ross (1973) and Harris and Raviv (1978), which seem to me to require too much information and more interference (knowledge of actual output; ability to set a "standard output," "target," or "norm") than is consistent with the intent of workers' self-management. Matters would be different in the *ex post* case. If price is known to the LMF before effort is committed, it is only reasonable to assume that the same information is known to the bank. This informa-tion may in fact be essential, and, indeed, the bank must know the distribution of the price itself. While the bank might use it to monitor effort, it does not need to under the form of contract to be proposed, whence I shall not explore the possibility.

The object is to find an incentive-compatible risk-sharing

form of contract between the LMF and the bank. It is natural to consider this as a principal–agent problem. For some years, the "first-order approach" has been commonly adopted in discussion of principal–agent problems. That is, the agent is to choose the action, unobservable to the principal, who is to set the contract optimal to him subject to the agent's utility not falling below some specified level (transfer earnings) and his first-order condition for the income–effort choice being satisfied. We now know, however, that this approach may be unsatisfactory (see Grossman and Hart, 1983 and works cited therein, particularly, of course, those of Mirrlees). The difficulties associated with the first-order approach are, in this instance, avoided in a simple and apparently "natural" fashion. Assume that the bank is required to meet only some break-even or minimum-profit condition. Consider the bank as "agent" and let the utility-maximizing LMF be the principal. In this (slightly unconventional) formulation, it is the principal who chooses the action (effort) unobserved by the agent. It is easy to see that the LMF will choose a maximal point for itself. It is shown in section 12.4 below that there may be more than one point at which its first-order conditions are satisfied, but that it will have no difficulty in choosing the best.

I assume, with Miyazaki and Neary (1983), that the bank is risk-neutral, and therefore need only be concerned that the contract generate the required expected profit. Plausible general-equilibrium conditions for Illyria would suggest that banks maximized profit, whence a "going rate" may be taken for partial-equilibrium analysis, and that members of LMFs got no more than their transfer earnings, whence it is immaterial, except for mathematical tractability, which we consider as principal and which as agent. For the present limited partial-equilibrium purposes, the approach outlined above seems both natural and tractable. (Some reason for thinking that banks in the ELMF should not themselves be LMFs was given in section 11.4 above.)

In Miyazaki and Neary (1983) LMF membership is denoted N, and the number working in any state is $n \leq N$. Miyazaki and Neary consider the optimal contract between members (the intra-LMF contract) which maximizes expected utility when the possibility of lay-off $(n < \mathcal{N})$ in some states is taken into account. They also consider the case in which the LMF can make members' incomes state-invariant by smoothing arrangements with a risk-neutral creditor. (It turns out that the famous perverse responses disappear.) Perfect smoothing, as was argued above, introduced the moral hazard problem whence this chapter is addressed to the question of coinsurance. I assume throughout that membership is fixed and fully employed. Low values of effort in the *ex post* case (it is fixed in the *ex ante* case) could be interpreted as short-time, a substitute for lay-off. A fully general treatment would, of course, combine both approaches, but I do not attempt it here. Apart from some comments in section 12.6 below the analysis is also entirely partial equilibrium. A general-equilibrium treatment would have to solve the problem of allocation of members between LMFs, presumably using equality of expected utilities as the equilibrium condition. For present purposes, it seems that little is lost by neglecting the problems associated with choice of $\mathcal{N}$ and n.

12.3   The model: the LMF–bank contract

In section 12.1 above, the only financial structure associated with (12.1) and stochastic p was 100 percent bond finance. There are other possibilities.[4] Thus suppose that the workers themselves own all the capital. Note that $r = v(i + \delta)$, where v is the price of a unit of k, i the interest rate and δ the depreciation rate, is the implicit rate that the LMF should charge itself for the use of capital. Clearly, the target rk need be attained only "on average": the LMF can hold reserves and do its own income smoothing. Now, if workers do own non-human capital, it is elementary that they should place it where its return is not perfectly correlated with that on their human capital ("don't force them to put all their eggs in one basket": see section 10.2 above). Full "self-financing" in this sense would also suggest the absence of a useful capital market and obvious difficulties over the allocation of capital. If, on the other hand, the LMF cannot smooth out of its own reserves, the reserves needed must be borrowed. Then the terms on which they are to be borrowed are to be investigated.[5] Development of an appropriate set of rules (a contract) is the subject of this chapter.

Since it has already been assumed that the LMF achieves a cooperative solution, we may write the production function $f(k,e)$ (since n is assumed to be constant, it may be suppressed). All that we need is $f_k, f_e > 0, f_{kk}, f_{ee} < 0$, and the assumption that total effort, e, is increasing in the effort of each individual, e_i: there is no need to specify the precise relationship between e and e_i. It is also assumed (see above) that all members have identical state-independent von Neumann–Morgenstern utility functions. For convenience, I also assume additive separability in this chapter, i.e., $U(y_i, e_i) = u(y_i) - v(e_i), \forall_i$, with standard properties.

A contract between LMF and bank must have the properties that

(1)   there is "enough" coinsurance to deal with the moral hazard problem, since
(2)   the bank does not monitor effort, and
(3)   workers maximize expected utility, while
(4)   the bank satisfies its minimum expected profit constraint.

I shall make no search here for an "optimal" (Second-Best) contract, but confine myself to linear fee schedules. This is done partly for reasons of tractability, partly because my main object is to show that there do exist incentive-compatible risk-sharing contracts which may be chosen by a viable but risk-averse LMF, and that such a contract may require so little information that it may be implementable.

Some form of share-cropping or profit-sharing[6] will provide coinsurance. Assume that the bank itself faces a known rate of interest r_0, and assume further that its minimum profit constraint is zero (break-even). It may lend to the LMF subject to its expected return being r_0. Since members of the LMF are risk-averse, some, but not complete, smoothing (guaranteed wages) is to be allowed. This suggests that the bank provides a mix of bond and (non-voting) "equity" capital while LMF members receive a mix of a base wage and a share in net revenue. The financial structure is described by two equations:[7]

$$y_i = w + \frac{s}{n} \{pf(k,e) - wn - rk\} \tag{12.2}$$

and

$$E[\pi] = E[(1-s)\{pf(k,e) - wn - rk\} + rk] - r_0 k = 0. \tag{12.3}$$

Notation:

> w is the base or fall-back wage, $0 \leq w < E[y]$
> s $(0 \leq s \leq 1)$ is the LMF's share in net profit
> r $(0 \leq r \leq r_0)$ is the bond rate to the LMF (writing two interest rates is notationally easier than dividing capital, k, into two components, and has no analytical consequences)[8]

(12.2) and (12.3) require more explanation. Assume that p has support in the interval $0 < \underline{p} \leq \underline{p} \leq \bar{p} < \infty$. It is possible that, at the lower end of this interval, the term $pf(k,e) - wn - rk$ is negative. As written, (12.2) and (12.3) suggest that members of the LMF share in the losses – i.e. that $y_i < w$ for low realizations of p. Members would clearly prefer that w be genuinely a guaranteed minimum, i.e. that (12.2) be replaced by

$$y_i = \begin{cases} w \text{ if } p \text{ is such that } pf(k,e) - wn - rk \leq 0 \\ w + \frac{s}{n} \{pf(k,e) - wn - rk\} \text{ otherwise.} \end{cases} \tag{12.4}$$

This is perfectly possible provided that the bank's constraint, (12.2), is met. It only requires that s or w be smaller, or r higher (or any combination of these) than would otherwise be the case. In the *ex ante* case considered here I shall confine myself to (12.2), as though negative net revenues were not possible.

Given that n is fixed, a contract, which may be written $\theta = \{w,r,s,k\}$, is an agreement by bank and LMF on the values of w,r,s,k, all of which must be chosen before the realization of p is known. The bank cannot monitor e itself, but clearly cannot agree to a contract without some knowledge of how e is determined.

The question is whether the LMF, which would prefer perfect smoothing ($s = 0$ and w guaranteed at a value higher than in the coinsurance case) will in fact agree to an interior solution ($0 < s < 1$). We can anticipate most of the answer to this question before proceeding to the details of the *ex ante* case. First, notice that, in order to be viable, the LMF must be able to satisfy (12.3), the bank's break-even constraint. Next, at $s = 0$, the bank will not sign a contract (provide any capital) whence members' utilities will be $U(0,0)$ (or perhaps the utility of some alternative employment, $\bar{U}$, say). Now there clearly exist strictly positive pairs, y,e, such that $U(y,e) > U(0,0)$ (and $\bar{U}$). That these values are consistent with (12.3) cannot possibly be guaranteed: the LMF might be potentially viable but not preferred. We can, however, say that, if the LMF is viable and preferred, $s = 0$ is excluded. Similarly, $s = 1$ is excluded. At $s = 1$ the bank's constraint collapses to $r = r_0$, as in the original Ward model, and a risk-averse LMF will disprefer this contract to a viable interior solution (some smoothing).

12.4 A two-stage solution

Let us now examine the details of the *ex ante* case, in which effort must be determined before the realization of price is known. It is convenient to adopt a two-stage procedure. The first step is to derive the supply function of effort conditional on the contract $\theta = \{w,r,s,k\}$, and the second to determine the contract itself, given conditional effort supply. The first step is therefore

$$\max_e E\left[u\left\{w + \frac{s}{n}(pf(k,e) - wn - rk) - v(e)\right\}\right]. \quad (12.5)$$

Here subscripts i on u, v, and e have been dropped. The assumptions made on the production function, together with the assumption that all members have identical utility functions, make it possible to do this to avoid clutter without loss of information. Conditional effort supply is the e^* that satisfies

$$\frac{s}{n}f_e E[u'(y)p] - v'(e) = 0. \quad (12.6)$$

Let (12.6) be solved by $e^* = e(w,r,s,k)$. It is immediate from (12.6) that $e^* = e(w,r,o,k) = 0$: no incentive, no effort! Thus, if there is a solution, it is an interior solution. To explore this, we need the comparative static properties of $e(\cdot)$. (Strictly, we perhaps need only $\partial e^*/\partial s$, but for completeness, all comparative static properties are derived.) A sufficient second-order condition for the maximization of (12.5) is

$$\frac{s}{n}f_{ee}E[u'(y)p] + \frac{s}{n}f_{e}E[u''(y)p\partial y/\partial e] - v'' < 0$$

where $\partial y/\partial e = sn^{-1}pf_e$. On the assumptions made, this is satisfied everywhere in $s\varepsilon[0,1]$. The comparative static properties of $e^* = e(w,r,s,k)$ are displayed in Table 12.1.

We may now proceed to the second stage of our solution. The LMF has yet to choose the optimal values of $\theta = \{w,r,s,k\}$, subject to the bank's break-even constraints, but we have the LMF's conditional effort supply, $e^*(\theta)$. (Use of $e^*(\theta)$ clearly amounts to adopting the "first-order approach," discussed in section 12.2 above, although it has been convenient to reverse the usual roles of principal and agent. Difficulties of non-existence or multiplicity of solutions are discussed in section 12.5 below.) We might treat this as another constraint, but it is easier to substitute it into $U(y,e)$ to obtain $u(y(\theta)) - v(e(\theta))$ as the LMF's maximand. Writing $\beta = E[p]$, and recalling the bank's constraint (12.3) in the *ex ante* case, we may form the Lagrangean

$$L(\theta,\lambda) = E\left[u\left\{w + \frac{s}{n}(pf(k,e^*) - wn - rk)\right\} - v(e^*)\right]$$
$$- \lambda[(1-s)\{\beta f(k,e^*) - wn\} + srk - r_0k]. \quad (12.7)$$

We should set

$$\frac{\partial L(\theta,\lambda)}{\partial\theta_i} = E\left[u'(y)\frac{\partial y}{\partial\theta_i}\right] - v'(e^*)\frac{\partial e^*}{\partial\theta_i}$$
$$- \lambda E\left[\frac{\partial\pi}{\partial\theta_i} + \frac{\partial\pi}{\partial e^*}\frac{\partial e^*}{\partial\theta_i}\right] = 0. \quad (12.8)$$

Table 12.1

Variable	Coefficient	Sign of partial derivative of $\overset{*}{e}=e(w,r,s,k)$ at		
		$s=0$	$s=1$	$0<s<1$
dw	$\dfrac{s}{n}f_e E[u''(y)(1-s)p]$	0	0	<0
dr	$-\dfrac{s}{n}kf_e E[u''(y)(1-s)p]$	0	>0	>0
ds	$\dfrac{s}{n}f_e E\left[pu''(y)\dfrac{1}{n}\{pf(k,e)-wn-rk\}\right]$			
	$+\dfrac{1}{n}f_e E[u'(y)p]$	>0	$?$	$?$
dk	$\dfrac{s}{n}f_e E\left[u''(y)\left(\dfrac{s}{n}pf_k-r\right)p\right]$			
	$+\dfrac{s}{n}f_{ek}E[u''(y)p]$	0	$?$	$?$

The four equations in (12.8), set out as (12A.1)–(12A.4) in Appendix A to this chapter (pp.144–145), together with the constraint, determine the LMF's "demands," w^*,r^*,s^*,k^*. These equations, with some discussion, are given in Appendix A to this chapter, but they add nothing essential here. The main point is already established: if the LMF is viable and a solution exists we shall have $s\varepsilon(0,1)$.

12.5 Existence and uniqueness

It is now time to consider more systematically the relationship between this approach and the usual first-order approach, the existence or otherwise of a solution, and the possibility of multiple solutions. Consider Figure 12.1 (based on Figure 1 in Grossman and Hart, 1983). y on the horizontal axis is, of course, the income of LMF members, and e their effort. Let us start by illustrating preferences. The direction of preference is, of course, South East. It is easy to see that, on the standard assumptions made on u'' and v'', the "no-worse-than" sets are convex. The first-order approach requires $U \geq \bar{U}$ (transfer earnings), illustrated in Figure 12.1, and $u'/v' = 1$. As Grossman and Hart point out, the locus of points where the latter condition is satisfied may be "wriggly," some parts of it may dominate others, and at the principal's "best" attainable point on $\bar{U}$ it might not hold at all.

To illustrate the present approach we need an effort supply function and a contract locus. To construct these, let us suppose that all elements of θ except s are held constant (if all elements of θ are fixed the contract locus is a single point). Everything else constant, y is increasing in s, so we may consider the effort supply function $e(s)$. From Table 12.1 we know that $e = 0$ at $s = 0$, where $y = w$, and that the supply function has a positive slope at that point. After that, its comparative static properties are not determined. I have chosen to illustrate a supply function with a region of positive slope that becomes backward bending at higher y, e values.

Now for the contact locus. Increasing s (or y) alone reduces $E[\pi]$, whence, if the constraint is to hold, increased y must be accompanied by increased e: the contract locus, $C(s)$, must have a positive slope in y–e-space. It is straightforward, if tedious, to calculate that its slope must be increasing in y. The intuitive explanation is simply diminishing returns, $f_{ee} < 0$: as y and e increase, e must increase at an increasing rate if the increase in revenue is to satisfy the constraint. Is $C(s)$ more or less "bendy" than $e(s)$, that is, if it intersects it at all, does it do so from "within" or "without"? On the assumptions made, there is no means of telling, nor does it seem to matter. I have arbitrarily chosen to illustrate a pair, $C_2(s)$ and $e(s)$, such that the former intersects from within.

There are clearly several possibilities. The first is that there is no solution: $C_1(s)$ nowhere touches $e(s)$. We cannot conclude that the LMF is not viable, since elements of θ other than s have

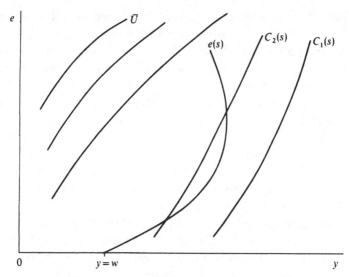

Figure 12.1   Contract loci and an effort supply function

been arbitrarily fixed. Let us suppose that, at some other values of w,r,k, we have $C_2(s)$: the LMF is viable. There are now two solutions. This is, however, no cause for embarrassment: the LMF, as principal, picks the one it prefers. There may, too, be an infinite set of solutions ($C(s)$ and $e(s)$ coincide over some range). For the same reason, this causes no embarrassment. And there may, of course, be a unique solution (as things are drawn in Figure 12.1, this would have to be a point of tangency between $C(s)$ and $e(s)$, but this is not in general necessary).

Finally, we may conjecture that general equilibrium in Illyria would be signalled by a unique solution *on* $\bar{U}$; but exploration of general equilibrium is beyond the scope of this analysis.

12.6   Information and honesty

A contract is now a vector $\theta^* = \{w^*, r^*, s^*, k^*\}$ that satisfies the LMF's demands and the bank's expected profit constraint. Since the LMF's demands are derived *under* that constraint, it appears that the bank need only announce (12.3) as its contract locus and accept any θ^* proposed by the LMF, which would indeed make its work easy. We have, however, still to ask if the LMF has any incentive to misrepresent its state (ask for a contract other than θ^*) and, if so, if the bank has any reasonable way of detecting the misrepresentation and enforcing an "honest" contract.

At least we do not have to worry about the supply of effort once the contract is signed: the shares system is incentive-compatible in that respect, and no monitoring is called for. What must concern us is the fact that the constraint really does bind. The innocuous interpretation is that the LMF merely wishes that the constraint were relaxed, i.e. that r_0 were lower. The worrying interpretation is that it has an incentive to overstate expected revenue $pf(k^*,e^*)$. If this does this, then in the "long run" the bank's break-even constraint will not be satisfied, and it will be forced to renegotiate the contract. It is easy to assume, as I did above, that the bank knows the distribution of the LMF's net revenue, but how, in fact, could it detect the fraud in the short run (since, by assumption, it cannot monitor p or e), or provide a disincentive to mendacity (or merely incompetent optimism)? There may exist some form of Second-Best contract which would make truth revelation by the LMF the dominant strategy, but I have not pursued the matter. Without such a contract, it looks as though, even in an ELMF, bankers will have to learn about their clients. It looks as though the contract will have to specify a duration (sample size) at the end of which it can be renegotiated not merely to break-even in future but to recoup past losses (repay gains). Evidently if this is not done the bank's contract-locus loses credibility: "bail-out" (in the sense of accepting $E[\pi] < 0$ as opposed to partial smoothing of y) destroys the system itself.

This, unfortunately, does not exhaust our informational difficulties. In ch. 11 we tried to provide an institutional structure such that the cooperative solution for the LMF was at least plausible. Now the LMF, or its manager, have to "know" $\theta^* = \{w^*,r^*,s^*,k^*\}$ or, since these are complete solutions, to know at least $e^*(w,r,s,k)$. The assumption that all members have identical utility functions should help. The limitation of contracts to linear structure is intended to help. We may assume by this time that the manager, at least, is familiar with the production function. Perhaps, if cooperative solutions are assured, the "representative" member can now speak for all, respond to the manager's "calling" of trial values of w,r,s,k, and allow the manager to construct some sort of schedule to take to the bank. I cannot say that I feel this to be very satisfactory.

12.7 General-equilibrium problems

So far, the existence of LMFs each with a given number of members, all having "the same" utility functions, has been taken for granted. The questions of exit and entry (coalition formation), the allocation of workers to LMFs and the implicit property rights of members, deserve more serious attention than, to my knowledge, they have yet had,[9] or will receive here. I will sketch only briefly the way in which a model by Kihlstrom and Laffont (1979) might be adapted to present purposes. Suppose for the moment that we can take the supply of effort as fixed: workers differ only in their degree of risk-aversion. Suppose also that they can be identified by an index $\alpha \varepsilon [0,1]$, where absolute risk-aversion is non-decreasing in α. Let there be an alternative safe occupation to membership in a risky LMF. Then an equilibrium allocation of workers between the safe occupation and membership would be a partition such that all workers less risk-averse than some $\bar{\alpha}$ were members and all workers not less risk-averse non-members; and associated with this partition would be an equilibrium pair, the safe wage and the risky return. If, in addition, LMFs (actual or potential) could be ranked according to their riskiness, a complete allocation would partition the workers among them. Indeed, in an "ideal" world (a continuum of LMFs as well as workers) the measure of α over the members of each LMF would be zero, justifying the assumption of identical utility functions.

Unfortunately, the riskiness of a LMF, as measured by the distribution of members' income, is not uniquely determined by "nature," or by the distribution of price: it also depends on the decisions made by the members and, in particular, on the size of the membership itself. I unfortunately do not see how to solve the general-equilibrium allocation problem where the riskiness of each LMF is endogenous.

When we introduce the supply of effort, matters become even more complicated. We can obviously construct measures of effort-aversion analogous to the common measures of risk-aversion, index workers by a measure of effort-aversion $\beta\varepsilon[0,1]$, and proceed to partition the labor force as in the pure risk case above. The analysis above shows that the effort level chosen by the LMF is not independent of its attitude to risk, while the division of the risk between LMF and bank is not independent of the attitude to effort. Thus we have to model the allocation jointly in α and β. This does not look easy.

The main point of this chapter is that, if there is risk in Illyria, then cooperative members must share some of it, at least in the absence of a complete set of futures markets. Satisfactory coinsurance requirements, like the cooperative solution itself, require more information than is very easily available.

Appendix A: The *ex ante* case

Equations (12.8) are:

$$\frac{\partial L}{\partial w} = E\left[u'(y)\left\{(1-s)+\frac{s}{n}pf_e\frac{\partial e^*}{\partial w}\right\}\right] - v'(e^*)\frac{\partial e^*}{\partial w}$$

$$- \lambda(1-s)\left\{pf_e\frac{\partial e^*}{\partial w}-n\right\}=0 \tag{12A.1}$$

$$\frac{\partial L}{\partial r} = E\left[u'(y)\frac{s}{n}\left\{pf_e\frac{\partial e^*}{\partial r}-k\right\}\right] - v'(e^*)\frac{\partial e^*}{\partial r}$$

$$- \lambda\left\{(1-s)pf_e\frac{\partial e^*}{\partial r}+sk\right\}=0 \tag{12A.2}$$

$$\frac{\partial L}{\partial s} = E\left[u'(y)\frac{1}{n}\left\{pf(k,e^*)-wn-rk+spf_e\frac{\partial e^*}{\partial s}\right\}\right]$$

$$- v'(e^*)\frac{\partial e^*}{\partial s}-\lambda\left\{(1-s)pf_e\frac{\partial e^*}{\partial s}-pf(k,e^*)+wn+rk\right\}=0 \tag{12A.3}$$

$$\frac{\partial L}{\partial k} = E\left[u'(y)\frac{s}{n}\left\{pf_k-r+pf_e\frac{\partial e^*}{\partial k}\right\}\right] - v'(e^*)\frac{\partial e^*}{\partial k}$$

$$-\lambda\left[(1-s)\hat{p}\left\{f_k+f_e\frac{\partial e^*}{\partial k}\right\}+sr-r_0\right]=0 \qquad (12A.4)$$

together with the constraint.

We have already seen that, at $s=0$, $e=0$ which is not acceptable to the bank. We also have here $\partial e^*/\partial w=\partial e^*/\partial r=0$ (Table 12.1). In this case (12A.1) yields $\lambda=-n^{-1}E[u'(y)]$. At $s=1$ the bank's constraint requires $r=r_0$.

Appendix B: The *ex post* case

1   In the *ex post* case, the realization of price is, of course, known before effort is committed, and it seems only reasonable to assume that price information is available to the bank as well as the LMF. Both bank and LMF must know the distribution of price. The effort supply function, similarly, is contingent as well as conditional. It follows that we now have to consider the possibility of prices so low that it is not worth supplying any effort. Clearly we wish the contract to be so structured that the shut-down, or "don't harvest," decision is taken on appropriate criteria.

2   We proceed, as before, in two stages. Optimal e is the value that solves

$$u'(y)\frac{s}{n}pf_e-v'(e)=0 \qquad (12B.1)$$

Let this be solved by $e=\eta(\theta,p)$. It is easy to see that the comparative static properties of contingent effort supply with respect to θ are those of conditional effort supply (see Table 12.1), but we now have to add the response to price. Partially differentiating (12B.1) with respect to price, we have

$$u'(y)\frac{s}{n}f_e+u''(y)\left(\frac{s}{n}\right)^2 pf(k,e)f_e. \qquad (12B.2)$$

The sign of (12B.2) is ambiguous, whence the supply curve of effort may be upward or backward sloping in p. (The perverse response that disappeared with perfect smoothing in Miyazaki and Neary, 1983 has reappeared as a possibility with imperfect (Second-Best) smoothing.) We may rearrange (12B.2) as

$$u''(y)\frac{s}{n}f_e\left[\frac{u'(y)}{u''(y)}+\frac{s}{n}pf(k,e)\right]. \qquad (12B.3)$$

F

The first term in the brackets is a (negative) measure of risk-aversion and the second is necessarily positive. It does not appear that much more can be said. It may, however, be worth adding that it does not follow from (12B.2) or (12B.3) that $\partial \eta(\theta,p)/\partial p$ is independent of $v(\cdot)$. A sufficient second-order condition is

$$\frac{s}{n}\left[u'(y)pf_{ee}+u''(y)\frac{\partial y}{\partial e}pf_e\right]-v''<0 \tag{12B.4}$$

where $\partial y/\partial e=sn^{-1}pf_e$.

It is immediate from (12B.1) that $s=0$ implies $e=0$. And again, $s=1$ implies that the LMF bears all the risk, whence we may be assured that, if a solution exists, $s^*\varepsilon(0,1)$.

Before turning to the second stage of the maximization problem (determining θ^*) it is necessary to consider the "don't harvest" decision. Following the *ex ante* case, we should have

$$y=w+\frac{s}{n}\{pf(k,\eta(\theta,p))-wn-rk\}. \tag{12B.5}$$

(12.B.5) implies that $e=0$ ("don't harvest") whenever the realization of p is such that the term in braces is non-positive (a sufficient but not necessary condition). Let it be zero at some $\tilde{p}$ where $p<\tilde{p}<\bar{p}$. In this case, members would receive w for doing no work (recall that, in the *ex ante* case, they had supplied e^* in any case, whence w is the minimal reward for effort). The solution is not to set $w=0$ (or some level of unemployment compensation): the "don't harvest" criterion implied by (12B.5) is wrong.

A capitalist employer would not harvest only if he could not satisfy $pq\geq\hat{w}n$, where $\hat{w}$ is a parametric wage rate, higher (for comparable technology, etc.) than the w considered here. Now $u(\hat{w})$ must exceed $v(e)$ if he is to get the job done, whence we must have $pq>nv(e)$. The decision is clearly independent of sunk costs, whether of the form rk or the bygone costs of planting, etc. Clearly, we do not wish the LMF's criterion to be "contaminated" by rk. Suppose for a moment that, if realized $p\varepsilon[p,\tilde{p}]$, the bank sets $r=0$. Then the member's income is $w(1-s)+sn^{-1}pf(k,\eta(\theta,p))$. The corresponding criterion for continuing to work is that there exists an $e=\eta(\theta,p)$ such that $u\{sn^{-1}pf(\cdot)\}>(v(e))$ or

$$u\{spf(k,\eta(\theta,\pi))\}>nv(\eta(\theta,p)). \tag{12B.6}$$

This is similar to, but of course not identical with, the capitalist criterion. For worker-managers, it is the utility of the share of the "profit" that matters, not the absolute profit itself. Nonetheless, the social cost of continuing to harvest is clearly $nv(e)$ in both cases and, for the work to have social pay-off, the benefit (however divided) must exceed this disutility.

If the bank is to "forgive" rk when $p \varepsilon [\underline{p}, \tilde{p}]$, r must be a function of p. We require

$$r(p) = \begin{cases} \text{const if } p > \tilde{p} \\ 0 \qquad \text{if } p \leq \tilde{p}. \end{cases} \qquad (12\text{B}.7)$$

Now the bank's constraint must become

$$(1-s)\{E[pf(k,\eta(\theta,p))] - wn\} + skE[r(p)] - r_0 k = 0. \qquad (12\text{B}.8)$$

The maximand for the second stage of the maximization (setting θ) similarly becomes

$$E[u\{w + sn^{-1}(pf(k,\eta(\theta,p) - wn - kr(p))\} - v(\eta(\theta,p))]. \qquad (12\text{B}.9)$$

We can set up the Lagrangian and proceed as before (see below). In setting the contract, r must be set at a constant (positive) level. In (12B.8) and (12B.9) we have the expected value of $r(p)$, which is necessarily lower than the (positive) value of $r(p)$.
$(E[r(p)] = \int_{\underline{p}}^{\tilde{p}} r(p)h(p)dp$ for any constant r, where $h(p)$ is the density function defined over the whole domain of p.) It follows that the value of r must be higher (and/or those of w, s, and k lower, in combination) than would be the case if rk were not to be forgiven at realized $p \leq \tilde{p}$.

Clearly the assumption that the bank knows realized price is essential in this case. It follows that the bank costlessly knows output and can infer effort. Since the contract is incentive-compatible, it does not need to "monitor" effort. The information problems in arriving at and enforcing an "honest" contract that we discussed above are reduced in the *ex post* case, but the bank *must* know the distribution of price.

Maximizing (12B.9) subject to (12B.8), with associated multiplier μ, we have

$$E\left[u'\left(y\right)\left\{1 - s + \frac{s}{n}pf_e \frac{\partial e^*}{\partial w}\right\} - v'(e^*)\frac{\partial e^*}{\partial w}\right]$$

$$- \mu(1-s)E\left[pf_e \frac{\partial e^*}{\partial w} - n\right] = 0 \qquad (12\text{B}.10)$$

$$E\left[u'(y)\frac{s}{n}pf_e\frac{\partial e^*}{\partial w} - k\frac{\partial E[r(p)]}{\partial r} - v'(e^*)\frac{\partial e^*}{\partial r}\right]$$

$$- \mu\left\{(1-s)E\left[pf_e\frac{\partial e^*}{\partial r}\right] + sk\frac{\partial E[r(p)]}{\partial r}\right\} = 0 \qquad (12\text{B}.11)$$

$$E\left[u'(y)\frac{1}{n}\left\{pf(k,e^*) - wk - r(p)k + spf_e\frac{\partial e^*}{\partial s}\right\} - v'(e^*)\frac{\partial e^*}{\partial s}\right]$$

$$- \mu E\left[(1-s)pf_e\frac{\partial e^*}{\partial s} - pf(k,e^*) + wn + r(p)k\right] = 0 \quad (12\text{B}.12)$$

$$E\left[u'(y)\frac{s}{n}\left\{pf_k - r(p) + pf_e\frac{\partial e^*}{\partial k}\right\} - v'(e^*)\frac{\partial e^*}{\partial k}\right]$$

$$- \mu E\left[(1-s)\left\{pf_k + pf_e\frac{\partial e^*}{\partial k}\right\} + sr(p) - r_0\right] = 0 \quad (12\text{B}.13)$$

together with the constraint.

e^* is now given by $\eta(\theta,p)$ rather than $e(\theta)$. In (12B.11) $\partial E[r(p)]/\partial r$ is $\int_{\underline{p}}^{\bar{p}} h(p)dp$. Remarks already made on the cases $s=0$ and $s=1$ apply here, too.

Appendix: The taxation of economic rent[1]

A.1 The suggestions of Sun Yat Sen (1929) and Harberger (1965)

I shall briefly consider here a scheme originally devised as a truth-revelation mechanism for tax purposes. I shall put a very narrow, possibly unjustified, interpretation on this scheme as one intended to elicit truth about the valuation of rent-yielding assets only, as distinct from other forms of income and wealth. The desire for non-distorting taxes makes the taxation of rent appealing; and a truth-revelation mechanism that allowed us to identify and value sources of rent would be particularly appealing. It unfortunately turns out that the truth-revelation mechanism to be considered works only in (impossibly) ideal information conditions; and cannot, in any case, be relied on to distinguish between rent and other forms of income.

Consider a largely agrarian, and poor, country in which the main tax base is land. Suppose that the distribution of land ownership is strongly skewed, so that there exists a small plutocracy of extremely wealthy land-owners. Appraisal and tax collection are delegated to a few poorly-trained officials, who are easily corrupted or intimidated by the wealthy. Contemplating this situation in China, Sun Yat Sen (1929) proposed a scheme of self-assessment: each land-owner should declare, for tax purposes, his own valuation of his property, subject to the condition that the government, if it thought the land under-valued, could buy it at the owner's valuation.

Contemplating an analogous situation in parts of Latin America, Harberger (1965) proposed (entirely independently, I believe) a variation on this scheme: *anyone* who thought the land under-valued should be able to purchase it, at the owner's valuation (plus perhaps some small "cushion"). It is quite possible that Sun Yat Sen thought of this tax scheme as a step towards the nationalization of land, which he might have wished and Harberger would not; but this is not my present concern. I shall confine myself to Harberger's variation of the scheme, with the proviso that the owner may at any time revise, upward or downward, his declared valuation without penalty.[2]

It must, I think, be admitted, that, at least at first sight, this scheme is immensely attractive. Self-valuation of the tax base is effectively superseded by market valuation, *provided* that cooperative behavior or collusion can be ruled out (which, at least in the case of a small landed class, may seem unlikely). In the absence of collusion, we have no need for any appraisers, inspectors, or indeed policemen at all (non-payment of tax is simply dealt with by automatic forfeiture, the property to be resold at market value by the government). Furthermore, rent is the one non-distorting tax base: if we could apply this scheme to all sources of rent, perhaps we could become "single-taxers" after all! Unfortunately, and without any consideration of possible magnitudes, this is not feasible. There are two obvious difficulties: first, not only the possible "corruption" of the scheme by threats, blackmail, and side-payments, but the difficulties presented by imperfect information more generally; second, the difficulty of "disentangling" a source of rent from "improvements." I consider first the first, and easier, of these two difficulties.

A.2 The possibility of side-payments

Suppose that a property worth V is declared at $D, V > D$. Assuming for the moment perfect information (an extreme assumption), a third party may address the owner to the following effect: "I have it in mind to make a purchase offer $P, V \geq P > D$, for your property. It will save you tax, and perhaps inconvenience if, instead of revising your declaration, you pay me some fraction, say α, of $P - D$, in which case I shall not register my offer." If the owner thinks that this is the only "blackmail" threat he is likely to receive then, so long as $\alpha < 1$, he saves money by paying. Any arbitrary "cushion" must be larger than $V - D$ for any owner for this to be false. If, however, a whole market is perfectly informed, we have, in effect, easy entry. Nothing can be gained by paying off one threat if another will be delivered tomorrow, and the owner's only recourse is to declare $D = V$. Honesty is indeed the best policy.

This seems easy: the scheme is not ruled out by threats, "dirty tricks," and side-payments. Consideration of recent literature on auctions[3] suggests, however, that matters are more complicated if information is not perfect, and that equilibrium, if it exists, may have some strange properties. (The literature on auctions is relevant, since Harberger's scheme amounts to an ongoing, or continuous, auction.) Consider first the case of common but uncertain information. All participants – potential bidders and the incumbent – have imperfect and uncertain information on which to base their estimates. The incumbent owner must declare a valuation, which is analogous to announcing a reserve price at the opening of an auction. His declared valuation is likely to be a function of his own valuation (quite possibly erroneous), the tax rate to be levied, his subjective estimate of the distribution of the estimates of others, and perhaps his attitude to risk. Caution alone suggests that he will under-state his valuation, at least a little. It is not entirely obvious that an equilibrium exists. A successful bidder may, or may not, suffer from the "winner's curse." The transaction would, in any case, reveal information additional to that conveyed by the original declared price. In a repeated game, which this is, the owner's strategy in declaring value may become obvious, in which case it may be inverted to allow potential bidders to estimate the owner's true valuation (which, again, may be mistaken). If information is genuinely asymmetric, matters are more complicated. There is some risk of a series of mistaken transactions and re-valuations. Since more information is revealed at each step, the process may be convergent; but it can hardly be maintained that this is a satisfactory mechanism for revealing the true valuation of a tax base.

This is discouraging. The second difficulty is worse.

A.3   The difficulty of disentanglement

The impossibility of "disentanglement" appears to be an insuperable obstacle to this scheme. Virtually all land *is* improved. As single-taxers, we do not wish to confuse the normal return to capital with that to the "indestructible power of the soil." To use market valuation for the base of a rent tax, it must be true that the source of rent is an identifiable, marketable, entity, separable in a legal and physical sense from any improvement. Consider an extreme case in which this is not true: a rent to human ability. There is no way in which the source of this rent can be separated or "disentangled" from the individual, or any investment he has made in himself by way of training or practice. There is, of course, a way, quite otherwise, in which these rents can be extracted: a monopsony employer, be it of athletes, actors, or academics, can extract them (at least, if the borders can be closed). The impossibility of disentanglement is similarly insuperable in the cases of land, including housing, and extant assets such as oil fields and coal mines (unless, by historical accident, "mineral rights" have always been legally separate, and only leased to operators).

A.4   Natural resources and man-made sources of rent

Are we left, then, with any cases in which this seemingly delightful scheme can be employed – any cases, that is, in which disentanglement is feasible?

A possible answer is: "new natural resources," of which the most obvious examples are undrilled oilfields, any other yet unexploited mineral rights, and uncut forests (which may, indeed, be of new growth). In the USA the appropriate rights seem to belong to the state, and an auction system has been in place for many years. This is, of course, a "one-off" auction, for drilling or cutting rights, rather than the sort of "ongoing" auction envisaged by Harberger, but these auctions must have the desired effect of recovering at least some portion of the rent. Even here, however, the problem of disentanglement is not without difficulty. Exploration contributes essentially to information, and the rules must be designed to allow for this. And we should note that, if the tax were to be collected as a royalty rate, instead of as a lump-sum in a one-off auction, the highest bidder might be left without any incentive to extract the oil!

We must look further for a case of a rent-yielding asset which permits disentanglement without appraisal. I have been able to discover only one example of a separable source of rent which is attributable to the "machinations of man" rather than to the niggardliness of nature: brand-names or "logos." A brand-name is physically distinct from the production process and, indeed, this is often recognized in the market. Thus a producer may sell under more than one brand-name, or the owner of a brand-name purchase output from other producers to sell under his brand-name. Suppose, then, that all brand-names, logos, or trade marks had to be registered and self-valued for rent tax, distinct from corporation or profits tax, under Harberger rules. What might we expect?

In some cases a brand-name clearly carries a promise of quality which others would find it hard to match. Thus few people would be deceived by a Rolls Royce plaque on the nose of a Volkswagen, and Rolls Royce would probably not have to declare a very high valuation even to guard against mischief makers. In other cases, such as cosmetics, we are told that a large part of the price is to be attributed, not to production labor or materials, or to the monopoly of any special "know-how," but purely to selling costs. In this case the name may be a genuinely remunerative asset on its own. It is also said that in such a case the brand-name is likely to be a depreciating asset which requires maintenance by continued publicity. If so, the return is, of course, a quasi-rent, but there seems to be no obvious objection to market valuation. More important, if the consequence of successful puffing of a name is only to incur a greater tax liability it will be a less rewarding activity, and fewer resources will be devoted to it. Thus a Harberger rent-tax on brand-names that were not associated with particular quality would tend to erode its own base, in a manner which seems quite desirable.

There are other sources of rent not due to the niggardliness of nature but to successful business practice which seem quite unassailable by this means: for example, franchised dealerships and the monopoly attributable to pre-emptive entry.

Notes

1 Two preliminary matters

[1] A very strong statement of a utilitarian position has been offered by Mirrlees (1982). I offer no criticism here, but certainly invite the reader to examine it.

[2] In a famous paper on the monitoring of workers in a capitalist firm, Alchian and Demsetz (1972) suggested the shareholders as the final "monitors of the monitors." To anyone familiar with the long discussion of the consequences of the "divorce" between ownership and control, to which Adam Smith made a well known contribution, this may appear a little naive. Smith's distrust of agency was so profound that he could really approve only of organizations so small that no agency was required: all supervision and monitoring could be carried out by working owners or "co-partners." The problems of information and control *within* a large organization, which have been much discussed, are beyond the scope of this book. It may be remarked, however, that if (for example) a foreman "bends the rules" in return, say, for sexual favors (becoming a principal), a shareholder is more likely to learn of it, if at all, through the press than by more direct channels.

2 Extended preferences

[1] In writing this chapter, I have drawn heavily on joint work with David Donaldson. I am indebted to him for permission to do so, and even more for much helpful discussion over the years. I am similarly indebted to Søren Q. Lemche for his patience in explaining things to me, and to both for their comments on an earlier draft of this chapter.

[2] Collard's contribution deserves particular mention, since Edgeworth's remarks on this subject were buried in a footnote, p. 53 of his (1881), and he offered no proofs of his assertions, nor, indeed, any development at all.

[3] Mill was not writing of preferences as we now represent them, nor explicitly of prices, but some relevant passages from the *Essay on Liberty* may be worth quoting. "*Secondly*, the principle [of human liberty] requires liberty of tastes and pursuits; of framing the plan of our life to suit our own character; of

doing as we like, subject to such consequences as may follow: without impediment from our fellow-creatures, so long as what we do does not harm them, even though they should think our conduct foolish, perverse, or wrong." And, a little later: "The only freedom which deserves the name, is that of pursuing our own good in our own way, so long as we do not attempt to deprive others of theirs, or impede their efforts to obtain it. Each is the proper guardian of his own health, whether bodily, or mental and spiritual." One extreme school of criticism, of course, maintains that the set of purely self-regarding acts is, if not empty, at least negligible. From this position paternalism may be justified, but *who* is to be licensed to be paternalist *to whom*, and about *what*, may be hard to explain.

4 Rader's main concern seems to be to dispense with the assumptions of continuity and differentiability made by others.

4 First example: an externality problem

1 This chapter draws heavily on an earlier paper of mine, Archibald (1980). I am much indebted to the editors of the *Journal of Economic Behavior and Organization* for permission to reprint so much of it, and to Richard Day in particular for his help and comments at an earlier stage.

2 The effect of a tax on pollution is, of course, to lower the rents of polluters and to increase the rents of pollutees. Such distributional issues will not be discussed here.

3 Transaction costs may be serious. Consider the problem of noise outside hospitals. If the property right in noise were vested in drivers, they could insist that patients rose from their beds and came onto the street to bribe the drivers not to blow their horns. If the property right in quiet were vested in patients, drivers might enter the wards seeking someone with whom they might strike a bargain for permission to sound off. Either solution might be "efficient." The standard solution is to put up a notice saying "Hospital: quiet" (which is to invest the right in the patients) but to pay a policeman to enforce it from time to time (which is to make the right non-transferable). This really seems quite sensible.

4 A differentiable function $f(x)$ of a single variable is said to be pseudo-concave over a domain $\Gamma \subset R^1$ if, for any $x^1, x^2 \, \varepsilon \Gamma$,

$$f'(x^1)(x^2 - x^1) \leqq 0 \Rightarrow f(x^2) \leqq f(x^1).$$

The effect of pseudo-concavity is to exclude points of inflection with horizontal tangents at which the algorithm would "stick" but not convex "wriggles" in the function. The effect is thus to ensure, as in the case of concavity, that first-order conditions are sufficient. (See Mangasarian, 1969, p. 140.)

5 They model a firm divided into two departments, sales and production. The manager of the sales department maximizes profit (subject to a satisficing

parameter) by the same algorithm that is assumed here and, in the decentralized case, the chief engineer similarly minimizes production cost. It is shown (making appropriate concavity assumptions) that the process is convergent to the neighborhood of maximum profit if each manager in turn, having converged, "relaxes" (freezes) while the other searches again. In the present case, we have the tax clerk relaxing while first steel and then flowers search, steel also relaxing after convergence (there being no feed-back) while flowers search. Formally, this is a minor extension of Day and Tinney's (1968) model. As has been noted, flower output may oscillate while steel is converging (and will if output of x and z oscillate); but our concavity assumptions ensure that flowers will converge once steel has done so.

[6] It is common to display the usual first-order efficiency conditions (equality of MRS and MRT) in a convex economy by a two-stage maximization process. In the first stage the production possibility frontier is obtained by maximizing GNP for all non-negative price vectors subject to the technology and the resource constraints. In the second stage, the welfare of a (representative) consumer is maximized subject to the production possibility frontier as a constraint. To demonstrate the Second-Best problem, a distortion is introduced at this second stage. Let us substitute a one-stage maximization problem, maximizing welfare subject to the technological and resource constraints. The distortion may be introduced directly as a constraint at this stage. Then simple manipulation of the first-order conditions shows that, if the distortion is in a product market only, then Second-Best requires First-Best efficiency conditions in input markets. This is set out in detail in Allingham and Archibald (1975). For further discussion of the joint problem of externalities and Second-Best, see Archibald and Wright (1976).

5 Second application of the control process: Lerner's Problem

[1] Domar (1974) apparently thought that we should at least have to know the elasticity of demand. I doubt if that is to be taken too literally: it probably seemed to him a convenient parameterization of the sort of information needed to check (5.4). In any case, if the control works, this sort of prior information is unnecessary. I have already noted that I do not propose to offer a detailed history of this branch of the literature, but it should be recorded that Domar in fact suggested that revenue, $qf(q)$, be an argument of the reward function where I have written q. Tam (1981) pointed out that this could lead to difficulties at values of q at which marginal revenue is negative, and suggested replacing revenue with sales.

[2] See also Tam (1985), and, for other contributions to the literature following Domar (1974), Finnsinger and Vogelsang (1981) and (1982), and Gravelle (1983).

6 Third example of the control process: implementation of a Second-Best solution

1 This chapter is drawn largely from Archibald and Davidson (1983). I am very grateful to Russell Davidson for permitting me to use this work. He is not responsible for the interpretation I put on it here.

2 Blackorby, Davidson and Schworm (1991). See also Blackorby and Donaldson (1990).

3 Even if he does not, only a *monetary* effect can ensue, since the tax clerk (or the government) uses no resources. Obviously macroeconomic effects can be important in practice, but we can ignore them in this model because we are always on the production possibility frontier by the assumption of perfect factor markets.

4 If, instead of producer prices, it is a set of per-unit or *ad valorem* taxes that are held fixed by the tax clerk, then changes in the monopolist's price or output would in general change q and, therefore, also x and y. His demand function would then be different. An argument similar to the one presented, but more delicate in detail, still goes through to prove that a constraint in commodity-space describes the monopolist's behavior.

7 Two examples of the control process in a mixed economy

1 Warning: the Harris–Wiens iterative process has an awkward feature. If, at the first step ($t = 1$, say), Q^1 is set too low, and if the private firms "believe" the announced reaction function $q_0^1 = Q^1 - \sum_{i=1}^{n} q_i^1$, they will wish to over-produce, i.e. q_0^1 will have to be negative to support the price implied by the announced Q^1. To avoid the necessity of stockpiling by the public enterprise, "someone" must be clever enough to set Q^1 such that it "jumps" the interval in which q_0 is negative to the interval closer to Q^* (and accordingly further from any initial condition that we might expect the private oligopoly to satisfy) in which q_0 is positive. In my discussion of the reward function, it is assumed (optimistically) that this has been done.

2 Consider a simple adaptation of Domar's original scheme (1974), i.e. let the bonus depend on the value (of industry sales now, of course) rather than the quantity. Thus let $R = \delta\Pi_0 + \mu D(Q)Q$ (neglecting the constant). It is straightforward to compute that, to satisfy the sign conditions on $\partial R/\partial Q$, we require

$$\mu[\text{Industry marginal revenue}] + \delta D'(Q)q_0 = 0$$

It is quite possible that the sign of industry marginal revenue is negative, or changes during the adjustment process, whence I have not pursued this alternative. It does have the attractive property that, after a little manipulation, one finds that μ/δ can be written $-S(1+\eta)/\eta$, where S is the share, q_0^*/Q^*, of the public enterprise and η is the elasticity of the industry demand curve at Q^*, whence we can compute the relative weights to be attached to profits and sales in the reward function for plausible (or merely illustrative) values of S and η.

9 Non-convexity and optimal product choice

1   The principal sources are, of course, Lancaster (1966); (1971); (1975); (1979); and Gorman (1980/1956). To the best of my knowledge, Lancaster, in his (1975) and (1979), was the first to draw attention to the connection between equity, efficiency, and choice of product, which is the subject of this chapter. I am, however, unable to follow his analysis, for reasons given in Archibald, Eaton, and Lipsey (1986), and Archibald and Eaton (1989). I am much indebted to Curtis Eaton for discussion of questions addressed here.

2   It has at least been shown that the problems are not insuperable. See Morey (1981) and Burton (1989).

3   His model was discussed in Archibald, Eaton, and Lipsey (1986), whence I may be brief here.

4   It is natural to look for analogies in the literature on spatial economics, particularly since it has been argued (Archibald and Eaton, 1989) that the monopolistic competition (product differentiation) and spatial economic theory may be usefully seen as two very similar but distinct applications of characteristics theory. Eaton and Wooders (1985) obtain striking asymptotic results for a spatial model, particularly that if average cost functions are U-shaped, free-entry equilibrium is competitive and socially optimal, whereas if there are no diseconomies of scale even large economies remain imperfect. Unfortunately we cannot rely here on an analogy with their results, since their "scale" experiments are not scale experiments as normally defined at all. Their fixed cost is a once-for-all set-up or product development cost. Variable costs are incurred to employ a homogeneous input. We might think of the variable input as composed of uniform "doses" of labor and capital, in Ricardian fashion, but must remember that what is fixed is not land: diminishing returns are possible but not implied. It is perhaps best to substitute "outlay" for "scale" in reading their paper.

10 Pareto-improvements and cooperatives

1   This is the expression used by Meade (1986, p. 117). He discussed so many of the questions taken up in Part IV of this book that, rather than clutter the text with detailed references, I make this one acknowledgement to his contribution.

2   I depart here from the rule proposed in section 10.2 above, to avoid anecdote, example, and indeed, any discussion of realized types, in order to mention the work by Kerr (1984) on innovation by capitalist firms within a (fairly) competitive market structure. Kerr is concerned with the diffusion of

an innovation ("exotic," that is, imported, breeds of bull) in the Canadian beef-raising industry. I mention this work for two reasons. First, each breeding bull is a separate entity, or factor of production. If each is treated as unique, estimation of the determinants of (auction) prices is clearly impossible. To treat the bulls, on the other hand, as a homogeneous factor of production is clearly counter-factual. This problem is solved by estimating the demand for the genetic *characteristics* embodied in bulls. The second reason is rather more to the immediate purpose. A quite unregulated market seems to have "worked" in the sense that diffusion was reasonably rapid and that the breeders (importers) seem to have responded to the (imputed) shadow prices of the characteristics. The beef-producing industry is highly competitive, the breeding industry less so because the import of exotic bulls is limited by regulation (non-tariff barriers) in such a way that there are clearly rents, or quasi-rents, to be had. One may think, in any case, that an innovation process left to the self-interested greed of "Canadian kulaks" has worked as well as the government has let it.

11 Achieving Pareto-efficiency in the LMF

[1] This chapter draws heavily upon Archibald and Neary (1983). I am greatly indebted to Hugh Neary for permission to use the work, and for discussion and comment.

[2] Thus perhaps reminding one uncomfortably of German practice in occupied countries in the Second World War, or of the inter-war British colonial practice of bombing villages whose authorities had not surrendered a wanted man.

[3] MacLeod (1988) suggests an ingenious rule for the selection of the weights α_i of (11.1) above: that the resulting allocation induce no envy. I commented unfavorably in ch. 2 on the introduction of "productivity ethics" to "save" the notion of fair allocations in production economies; but it seems quite possible that the members of an LMF should be sufficiently homogeneous in skill and effort-aversion for this to be a plausible approach.

12 Risk-sharing in Illyria (or the ELMF)

[1] For helpful discussion, and comments on a much earlier version of this chapter, I am greatly indebted to Erwin Diewert, J.M. Malcolmson, Hugh M. Neary, David Robinson, and W. Craig Riddell.

[2] As has been done in several papers (e.g. Paroush and Kahana, 1980; Hey, 1981; Miyazaki and Neary, 1988).

[3] Crop-planting is an obvious example of the *ex ante* case, and harvesting may be an example of the *ex post* case. If prices do not change much from week to week, much of manufacturing may be more or less *ex post*. I say "more or less" since strictly we should probably say only that the priors are restricted to a relatively small subset of the domain before effort is committed. The

"real world" probably offers awkward mixtures of the two cases, but I shall consider here only the polar cases.

⁴ Hey (1981) suggested that the LMF have access to a futures market in which it might hedge. (Cf. Lerner's, 1944, discussion of "counter-speculation" in his socialist economy.) Leaving aside well known requirements for the existence of futures markets (homogeneous or easily graded products, etc.), the question is: in a socialist economy, who would speculate, with whose funds, and under what incentive structure? Until some answer is provided, this "solution" to the problem of risk-sharing in the ELMF must be regarded as fanciful. We know, however, that a major obstacle to the attainment of efficiency in our "ideal" capitalist economy may be the absence of a complete set of markets, and it seems at least possible that the difficulty is greater in the ELMF.

⁵ Although this chapter is concerned with an LMF in an ELMF, the problem considered is not exclusively Illyrian. It is easy to imagine a group of equity-owning company directors negotiating with their bank for smoothing arrangements, although ownership is entirely capitalist in form.

⁶ It is an ancient practice in sea-fishing that participants be rewarded on the "share" or "lay" system: so many shares for each crew member, perhaps varying with skill, so many for the captain, and "the boat's share": see Sutinen (1979). Sutinen's model differs from that suggested here in several ways: (1) the principal (captain) is risk-averse as well as the crew; (2) his expected utility is to be maximized subject to that of crew members not falling below the alternative (safe) level; (3) all capital is (implicitly) raised from a third party on a fixed-interest bond; (4) monitoring (of the crew by the captain) is built-in – there is no residual moral hazard.

⁷ This financial structure gives a linear fee structure, $w + sn^{-1}$ (net revenue) for the principal (rather than the agent). Ross (1973) has analyzed the variational problem involved in choosing a fee structure, and obtained the conditions on which a linear structure is optimal. As noted, I do not consider non-linear structures here.

⁸ This is easily checked. Write $k = k^b + k^e$ where k^b is bond capital and k^e equity capital. Then (12.1) and (12.3) become

$$y = w + \frac{s}{n}\{pf(k,e) - wn - r_0 k^b\}$$

and

$$E[\pi] = (1-s)\{pf(k,e) - wn - r_0 k^b\} + r_0 k^b - r_0 k = 0.$$

Clearly the two schemes are actuarially identical, and identical in all respects if variables are chosen such that $r/r_0 = k^b/k$. Strictly, the effective interest rate to the LMF should be $i = v(r_0 + \delta)$ where v is the price of a unit of capital and δ the depreciation rate. For present purposes, this may be safely neglected. Multiplying (12.2) by n, adding (12.3), and adding $r_0 k$, the accounts can be seen to "add up." After each realization of p the bank of course gets $(1-s)$ times realized net revenues rather than the expectation.

[9] But see Ichiishi (1977). Ichiishi is concerned with the existence of competitive equilibrium in a (non-stochastic) coalition economy, and to show that the equilibrium is in the core.

Appendix

[1] I am greatly indebted to my colleagues Ken Hendricks and Goufu Tan for their comments on an earlier draft of this Appendix. They have removed many errors, but have no responsibility for those that may remain.

[2] Nuti (1988) has suggested that a version of Harberger's scheme might be applied to the managers of Soviet-style enterprises. Thus each manager would be required to post a valuation on the assets of his enterprise. Nuti's object is to encourage takeover by other enterprises of under-valued assets. He does not seem to be aware of the contributions of Sun Yat Sen or Harberger, nor of the difficulties discussed below.

[3] There is now a substantial theoretical and empirical literature on auctions, prompted in part by Vickrey's (1961) discovery of the "second-price" auction, in part by US experience. There are admirable surveys in Milgrom (1989) and Smith (1987). My own attention was first drawn to the US example by Leland (1978). This literature emphasizes and illuminates the roles of information and attitude towards risk.

Bibliography

Agassi, Joseph 1960 "Methodological Individualism." *British Journal of Sociology*, 11: 224–70.

Alchian, A.A. and Demsetz, H. 1972 "Production, Information Costs and Economic Organization." *American Economic Review*, 62: 777–95.

Allingham, M.G. and Archibald, G.C. 1975 "Second Best and Decentralization." *Journal of Economic Theory*, 10: 157–73.

Archibald, G.C. 1980 "Adaptive Control of Some Producer–Producer Externalities." *Journal of Economic Behavior and Organization*, 1: 81–96.

Archibald, G.C. and Davidson, Russell 1983 "Second Best and Stepwise Control." University of British Columbia, *Discussion Paper*, 83-23.

Archibald, G.C. and Donaldson, David 1976a "Non-paternalism and the Basic Theorems of Welfare Economics." *Canadian Journal of Economics*, 9: 492–507.

1976b "Paternalism and Prices," in M.G. Allingham and M.L. Burstein (eds.), *Resource Allocation and Economic Policy*. London: Macmillan.

1979 "Notes on Economic Equality." *Journal of Public Economics*, 12: 205–14.

Archibald, G.C. and Eaton, B. Curtis 1989 "Two Applications of Characteristics Theory," in George R. Feiwel (ed.), *The Economics of Imperfect Competition and Employment*. London: Macmillan.

Archibald, G.C., Eaton, B.C. and Lipsey, R.G. 1986 "Address Models of Value Theory," in Joseph E. Stiglitz and G. Frank Mathewson (eds.), *New Developments in the Analysis of Market Structure*. Cambridge, MA: MIT Press for the International Economics Association.

Archibald, G.C. and Neary, H.M. 1983 "Achieving Pareto-Efficient Outcomes in the Labour-Managed Firm." University of British Columbia, *Discussion Paper*, 83-25.

Archibald, G.C. and Wright, Colin 1976 "Alternative Solutions for the Control of a Production Externality in a General Equilibrium Model." *Economica*, 43: 391–403.

Arrow, Kenneth J. 1951a "An Extension of the Basic Theorems of Classical Welfare Economics," in J. Neyman (ed.), *Proceedings of the Second Berkeley Symposium on Mathematical Statistics and Probability*. Berkeley: University of

California Press. Reprinted in 1986 *Collected Papers of Kenneth J. Arrow: General Equilibrium*. Cambridge, MA: Belknap Press.

1951b *Social Choice and Individual Values*. New Haven and London: Yale University Press.

Arrow, Kenneth J. and Hurwicz, Leonid (eds.) 1977 *Studies in Resource Allocation Processes*. Cambridge: Cambridge University Press.

Baier, K. 1958 *The Moral Point of View: A Rational Basis of Ethics*. Ithaca: Cornell University Press.

Bain, Joe S. 1954 "Economics of Scale, Concentration and the Condition of Entry in Twenty Manufacturing Industries." *American Economic Review*, 64: 15–39.

Barone, E. 1908 "The Ministry of Production in the Collectivist State," in 1935 F.A. von Hayek (ed.), *Collectivist Economic Planning*. London: Routledge. (Reprinted from *Giornale degli Economisti*, 1908.)

Barzelay, Michael and Thomas, Lee R. III 1986 "Is Capitalism Necessary? A Critique of the Neoclassical Economics of Organization." *Journal of Economic Behavior and Organization*, 7: 225–34.

Baumol, William J. 1986 *Superfairness: Applications and Theory*. Cambridge, MA: MIT Press.

Baumol, W.J. and Oates, Wallace E. 1975 *The Theory of Environmental Policy*. Englewood Cliffs, N.J.: Prentice-Hall.

Besanko, David and Sappington, David E.M. 1987 *Designing Regulatory Policy with Limited Information*. Chur, Switzerland: Harwood.

Blackorby, Charles, Davidson, Russell and Schworm, William 1991 "The Validity of Piecemeal Second-best Policy." *Journal of Public Economics*, 6: 267–90.

Blackorby, Charles and Donaldson, David 1990 "A Review Article: The Case Against the Use of the Sum of Compensating Variations in Cost-benefit Analysis." *Canadian Journal of Economics*, 23: 471–94.

Blackorby, Charles, Primont, Daniel and Russell, Robert R. 1978 *Duality, Separability and Functional Structure: Theory and Economic Applications*. New York: North-Holland.

Brown, D.G. 1972 "Mill on Liberty and Morality." *Philosophical Review*, 81.
1973 "What is Mill's Principle of Utility?" *Canadian Journal of Philosophy*, 3.

Brown, D.J. and Heal, G.M. 1979 "Equity, Efficiency and Increasing Returns." *Review of Economic Studies*, 57: 571–85.
1980 "Two-part Tariffs, Marginal Cost Pricing and Increasing Returns in a General Equilibrium Model." *Journal of Public Economics*, 13:25–49.

Burton, Peter S. 1989 *Product Interactions and Rivalry among Multiproduct Firms: an Application of Characteristics Theory*. Unpublished Ph.D. thesis: University of British Columbia.

Collard, David 1975 "Edgeworth's Propositions on Altruism." *Economic Journal*, 85: 355–60.
1978 *Altruism and Economy*. Oxford: Martin Robertson.

Corlett, W.J. and Hague, D.C. 1954 "Complementarity and the Excess Burden of Taxation." *Review of Economic Studies*, 21 (1953–4): 21–30.

Day, Richard H. 1967 "Profit, Learning, and the Convergence of Satisficing to Marginalism." *Quarterly Journal of Economics* 81: 302–11.

1975 "Adaptive Processes and Economic Theory," in Richard H. Day and Theodore Groves (eds.), *Adaptive Economic Models*. London and New York: Academic Press.

Day, Richard H. and Groves, Theodore (eds.) 1975 *Adaptive Economic Models*. London and New York: Academic Press.

Day, Richard H. and Tinney, E.H. 1968 "How to Cooperate in Business without Really Trying: A Learning Model of Decentralized Decision Making." *Journal of Political Economy*, 76: 583–600.

Debreu, G. 1959 *Theory of Value*. New York: John Wiley & Sons.

Domar, Evsey D. 1974 "On the Optimal Compensation of a Socialist Manager." *Quarterly Journal of Economics*, 88:1–18.

Dow, Gregory K. 1986 "Control Rights, Competitive Markets, and the Labor Management Debate." *Journal of Comparative Economics*, 10: 48–61.

Eaton, B. Curtis and Lipsey, R.G. 1980 "Exit Barriers are Entry Barriers: the Durability of Capital as a Barrier to Entry." *Bell Journal of Economics*, 11: 721–9.

Eaton, B. Curtis and White, W.D. 1983 "The Economy of High Wages: An Agency Problem." *Economica*, N.S., 50: 175–82.

Eaton, B. Curtis and Wooders, Myrna Holtz 1985 "Sophisticated Entry in a Model of Spatial Competition." *Rand Journal of Economics*, 16: 282–97.

Edgeworth, Francis Ysidro 1881/1967 *Mathematical Psychics*. Reprint 1967. New York: Augustus M. Kelly.

Eswaran, Mukesh and Kotwal, Ashok 1984 "On the Moral Hazard of Budget-Breaking." *Rand Journal of Economics*, 5: 578–81.

Finnsinger, Jörg and Vogelsang, Ingo 1979 "A Regulatory Adjustment Process for Optimal Pricing by Multiproduct Monopoly Firms." *Bell Journal of Economics*, 10: 157–71.

1981 "Alternative Institutional Frameworks for Price Incentive Mechanism." *Kyklos*, 34: 338–404.

1982 "Performance Indices for Public Enterprises," in L.P. Jones (ed.), *Public Enterprise in Less Developed Countries*. Cambridge: Cambridge University Press.

1985 "Strategic Management Behavior Under Reward Structures in a Planned Economy." *Quarterly Journal of Economics*, 100: 263–9.

Gorman, W.M. 1980/1956 "A Possible Procedure for Analyzing Quality Differentials in the Egg Market." *Review of Economic Studies*, 47: 843–56.

Gravelle, H.S.E. 1983 "Alternative Institutional Frameworks for Price Incentive Mechanisms." *Kyklos*, 36: 115–20.

1985 "Reward Structures in a Planned Economy: Some Difficulties." *Quarterly Journal of Economics*, 100: 271–8.

Grossman, Sanford J. and Hart, Oliver D. 1983 "An Analysis of the Principal–Agent Problem." *Econometrica*, 51: 7–45.

Groves, Theodore 1976 "Information, Incentives, and the Internalisation of Production Externalities," in Steven A.Y. Lin (ed.), *Theory and Measurement of Economic Externalities*. New York: Academic Press.

Groves, Theodore and Loeb, Martin 1975 "Incentives and Public Inputs." *Journal of Public Economics*, 4: 211–26.

Guesnerie, Roger 1975 "Pareto Optimality in Non-Convex Economies." *Econometrica*, 43: 1–29.

Guesnerie, Roger and Laffont, Jean-Jacques 1978 "Taxing Price Makers." *Journal of Economic Theory*, 19: 423–55.

Hammond, Peter J. 1980 "Cost Benefit Analysis as a Planning Procedure." *Contemporary Economic Analysis*, 2: 221–49.

Harberger, Arnold C. 1965 "Issues of Tax Reform for Latin America", in *Fiscal Policy for Economic Growth in Latin America*, issued by the Joint Tax Program of the Organization of American States, Inter-American Development Bank and Economic Commission for Latin America. Baltimore: Johns Hopkins Press.

Harris, M. and Raviv, A. 1978 "Some Results on Incentive Contracts." *American Economic Review*, 68: 20–30.

Harris, Richard G. and Wiens, Elmer G. 1980 "Government Enterprise: An Instrument for the Internal Regulation of Industry." *Canadian Journal of Economics*, 13: 125–31.

Hart, O. 1979 "Monopolistic Competition in a Large Economy with Differentiated Commodities." *Review of Economic Studies*, 46: 1–30.

Heal, G.M. 1973 *The Theory of Economic Planning*. Amsterdam and New York: North-Holland and Elsevier.

Heller, Walter P. and Starrett, David A. 1975 "On the Nature of Externalities," in Steven A.Y. Lin (ed.), *Theory and Measurement of Economic Externalities*. London and New York: Academic Press.

Hey, John D. 1981 "Hedging and the Competitive Labor-Managed Firm under Price Uncertainty." *American Economic Review*, 71: 753–7.

Holmstrom, B. 1982 "Moral Hazard in Teams." *Bell Journal of Economics*, 13: 324–40.

Horvat, B. 1976 *The Yugoslavian Economic System*. White Plains, NY: Sharpe Inc.

Kerr, W.A. 1984 "Selective Breeding, Hereditable Characteristics and Genetic-based Technological Change in the Canadian Beef Cattle Industry." *Western Journal of Agricultural Economics*, 9: 14–25.

Kihlstrom, Richard E. and Laffont, Jean-Jacques 1979 "A General Equilibrium Entrepreneurial Theory of Firm Formation Based on Risk Aversion." *Journal of Political Economy*, 87: 719–48.

Ichiishi, Tatsuro 1977 "Coalition Structure in a Labour-Managed Market Economy." *Econometrica*, 45: 341–60.

Lancaster, K.J. 1966 "A New Approach to Consumer Theory." *Journal of Political Economy*, 74: 132–57.

1971 *Consumer Demand: a New Approach.* New York: Columbia University Press.

1975 "Socially Optimal Product Differentiation." *American Economic Review*, 65: 567–85.

1979 *Variety, Equity, and Efficiency.* New York: Columbia University Press.

Lange, Oscar 1936/7 "On the Economic Theory of Socialism." *Review of Economic Studies*, 4: 53–71 and 123–44.

Leibenstein, H. 1950 "Bandwagon, Snob, and Veblen Effects in the Theory of Consumer's Demands." *Quarterly Journal of Economics*, 64: 183–207.

Leland, Hayne 1972 "Theory of the Firm Facing Uncertain Demand." *American Economic Review*, 62: 278–91.

1978 "Optimal Risk Sharing and the Leasing of Natural Resources, with Application to Oil and Gas Leasing on the OCS." *Quarterly Journal of Economics*, 92: 413–37.

Lemche, S.Q. 1986a "Benevolent Preferences and Pure Public Goods." *Journal of Public Economics*, 30: 129–34.

1986b "Remarks on Non-paternalism and the Second Theorem of Welfare Economics." *Canadian Journal of Economics*, 19: 270–80.

Lerner, Abba P. 1944 *The Economics of Control.* London and New York: Macmillan.

Lipsey, Richard G. and Lancaster, K. 1957 "The General Theory of Second Best." *Review of Economic Studies*, 24 (1956–7): 11–32.

MacLeod, W. Bentley 1987 "Behavior and the Organization of the Firm." *Journal of Comparative Economics*, 11: 207–20.

1988 "Equity, Efficiency, and Incentives in Cooperative Teams." *Advances in the Economic Analysis of Participatory and Labor Managed Firms*, 3: 5–23.

Malinvaud, E. 1967 "Decentralized Procedures for Planning," in E. Malinvaud and M.O.L. Bacharach (eds.), *Activity Analysis in the Theory of Growth and Planning.* London: Macmillan.

Mangasarian, Olvi L. 1969 *Nonlinear Programming.* New York: McGraw-Hill.

Marglin, S.A. 1969 "Information in Price and Command Systems of Planning," in J. Margolis and H. Guitton (eds.), *Public Economics.* London: Macmillan for the International Economic Association.

Meade, James E. 1955a *Trade and Welfare.* London: Oxford University Press.

1955b *The Theory of Customs Unions.* Amsterdam: North-Holland.

1986 *Alternative Systems of Business Organization and of Workers' Remuneration.* London: Allen & Unwin.

Milgrom, Paul 1989 "Auctions and Bidding: a Primer." *Journal of Economic Perspectives*, 3: 3–22.

Mill, J.S. 1848 *Principles of Political Economy, with Some of Their Applications to Social Philosophy.* London: Parker. See J.M. Robson (ed.), *Collected Works of John Stuart Mill.* Toronto: University of Toronto Press (1965).

1859 *An Essay On Liberty.* London: J.W. Parker & Son.

Mirrlees, J.A. 1982 "The Economic Uses of Utilitarianism," in Amartya Sen and Bernard Williams (eds.), *Utilitarianism and Beyond*. Cambridge: Cambridge University Press.

Miyazaki, H. and Neary, H.M. 1983 "The Illyrian Firm Revisited." *Bell Journal of Economics*, 14: 259–70.

Morey, Edward R. 1981 "The Demand for Site-Specific Recreational Activities: a Characteristics Approach." *Journal of Environmental Economics and Management*, 8: 345–71.

Neary, Hugh M. 1987 "Incentive Compatible Planning with Incomplete Information." University of British Columbia, *Discussion Paper*, 87-25.

Nelson, Richard R. and Winter, Sidney G. 1982 *An Evolutionary Theory of Economic Change*. Cambridge, MA and London: the Belknap Press.

Nuti, D.M. 1988 "Competitive Valuation and Efficiency of Capital Investment in the Socialist Economy." *European Economic Review*, 32: 459–64.

Paroush, Jacob and Kahana, Nava 1980 "Price Uncertainty and the Cooperative Firm." *American Economic Review*, 70: 212–16.

Pazner, E.A. and Schmeidler, D. 1978 "A Difficulty in the Concept of Fairness." *Review of Economic Studies*, 41: 441–3.

Peacock, Sir Alan 1986 *Report of the Committee on Financing the BBC*, Chairman, Professor Sir Alan Peacock, DSC, FBA, Cmnd. 9824. London: HMSO.

Phillips, A.W. 1957 "Stabilisation Policy and the Time-forms of Lagged Responses." *Economic Journal*, 67: 265–77.

Pigou, A.C. 1920 *The Economics of Welfare*. London: Macmillan.

Popper, Sir Karl R. 1957 *The Poverty of Historicism*. London: Routledge & Kegan Paul.

Rader, J.T. 1980 "The Second Theorem of Welfare Economics When Utilities are Interdependent." *Journal of Economic Theory*, 23: 420–4.

Robertson, Sir Dennis H. 1956 *Economic Commentaries*. London: Staples Press.

Rosen, Robert 1975 "Biological Systems as Paradigms for Adaptation," in Richard H. Day and Theordore Groves (eds.), *Adaptive Economic Models*. London and New York: Academic Press.

Ross, Stephen A. 1973 "The Economic Theory of Agency: the Principal's Problem." *American Economic Review*, 63, 2: 134–9.

Sandmo, A. 1971 "On the Theory of Competitive Firm under Price Uncertainty." *American Economic Review*, 61: 65–73.

Simons, Henry Calvert 1944 "Some Reflections on Syndicalism." *Journal of Political Economy*, 52: 356–61.

Smith, Adam 1776 *An Inquiry into the Nature and Causes of the Wealth of Nations*. Dublin: Printed for Messrs. Whitesone Chamberlaine, W. Watson (etc.). Text references to 1937 Edwin Cannon (ed.), *An Inquiry into the Nature and Causes of the Wealth of Nations*. New York: Random House.

Smith, Vernon L. 1987 "Auctions," in J. Eatwell, M. Milgate and P. Newman (eds.), *The New Palgrave: a Dictionary of Economics*. London: Macmillan.

Spence, A.M. 1976 "Product Selection, Fixed Costs, and Monopolistic Competition." *Review of Economic Studies*, 43: 217–35.

Starrett, David A. 1972 "Fundamental Non-Convexities in the Theory of Externalities." *Journal of Economic Theory*, 4: 180–99.

Steiner, Peter O. 1961 "Monopoly and Competition in Television: Some Policy Issues." *Manchester School*, 29: 107–31.

Stephen, James Fitzjames 1874 *Liberty, Equality, Fraternity.* London: Smith, Elder & Co., 2nd edn.

Sun Yat Sen 1929 *The Three Principles of the People.* Shanghai: The Commercial Press.

Sussangkarn, Chal and Goldman, Steven M. 1983 "Dealing with Envy." *Journal of Public Economics*, 2: 103–12.

Sutinen, J.G. 1979 "Fishermen's Remuneration Systems and Implications for Fisheries Development." *Scottish Journal of Political Economy*, 26: 147–62.

Tam, Mo-Yin S. 1981 "Reward Structures in a Planned Economy." *Quarterly Journal of Economics*, 96: 111–28.

  1985 "Reward Structures in a Planned Economy: Some Further Thoughts." *Quarterly Journal of Economics*, 100: 279–89.

Taylor, Fred Manville 1929 "The Guidance of Production in a Socialist State." *American Economic Review*, 19: 1–8.

Ten, C.L. 1980 *Mill on Liberty.* Oxford: Clarendon Press.

Theil, Henri 1964 *Optimal Decision Rules for Government and Industry.* Amsterdam: North-Holland.

Varian, H.R. 1974 "Equity, Envy and Efficiency." *Journal of Economic Theory*, 9: 1–22.

  1975 "Distribution, Justice, Welfare Economics, and the Theory of Fairness." *Philosophy and Public Affairs*, 4: 223–47.

  1976 "Two Problems in the Theory of Fairness." *Journal of Public Economics*, 5: 249–60.

Vickrey, William 1961 "Counterspeculation, Auctions, and Competitive Sealed Tenders." *Journal of Finance*, 16: 8–37.

Ward, Benjamin 1958 "The Firm in Illyria: Market Syndicalism." *American Economic Review*, 48: 566–89.

Winter, Sidney 1969 "A Simple Remark on the Second Optimality Theorem of Welfare Economics." *Journal of Economic Theory*, 1: 99–103.

Index